WHAT OTHERS SAY . . .

M000311270

God is moving around the world in unprecedented ways to draw people to Jesus in what could be the greatest harvest of human souls in all of history. The big question is, "Will the Church be ready?" In her latest book, Pamela Christian tackles this challenging question with a combination of biblical wisdom, spiritual insight and practical tools to help the Church "Prepare for Harvest." This book describes the ripening harvest in great detail in contrast to the lack of readiness in the Church and then concludes with a set of practical things we can do to prepare for the next great awakening. I encourage every believer to study this book and get ready for the coming harvest!

—**Michael Brodeur**
Director: PastorsCoach.com

In her extensively researched book, *Prepare for the Harvest! God's Challenge to the Church Today,* Pamela Christian has written what amounts to a fabulous "white paper" about the state of the Christian church in America, its impact on our current culture and its future for reaching people with the Gospel. Pick up this book if you want to be immersed in facts, and not just hearsay to be better equipped to reach the lost for Christ!

—**Joe Battaglia**
President, Renaissance Communications; broadcaster, and author of
Unfriended: Finding True Community in a Disconnected Culture

As I read *Prepare for the Harvest! God's Challenge to the Church Today,* God showed me a picture of the author, Pamela Christian, in cap and gown, who had graduated with honors in God's School of the Spirit. Then throughout her book, Pam paints a very accurate picture of the state of the Church and it's not always a pretty picture to look at. Then I saw it—it was as if she had a pen in one hand and a Kleenex in the other hand she so deeply felt the emotions of God's revelation for this book and for His Church. This book includes many pages that carefully lay out the way things really are, and yet the author proceeds to write out the grace-filled prescriptions to address the malady today's Church struggles with. Finally, even if you don't read every single page, get this book, if only for the chapters that describe the many solutions for this generation, YOUR generation. God wants you to have a vision for where you can go with His help. Carry on! Prepare for the Harvest!

—Steve Shultz,

Founder, The Elijah List and Elijah Streams TV program

This new book by Pamela Christian is a manual for new believers as well as the more seasoned Christian. It lays bare the truth about the church today and gives an in-depth instruction of the plan of God for our lives in this difficult season. It is inspirational as we know that the truth will set us free. Only when we understand the circumstances can we move forward to apply the biblical remedies that will help us ascend to the challenges that God is calling us to engage therein. This book will assist you in doing just that.

—Erin Flynn-Clark,

Founder of Truth Be Told Prophetic Ministries, ordained prophet and pastor, international speaker, published author, producer of worship music and faith-based films

God promises His church will never fail and God calls His church to be obedient to the commission "Go make Disciples" (Matthew 28-19-20) and to be prepared for the harvest (Matthew 9:37). However, how can a diluted, superficial faith stand up against the current wicked, immoral, times? Pam Christian's wonderful book helps to re-direct the body of Christ to become stronger in faith and deeds; applying the word of God in order to meet the ever-increasing evil cultural onslaught. God is calling His church for battle and Pam's book details a battle plan for success!

—Lee Ann Mancini,
Author and Executive Producer of Sea Kids TV Series and
Adjunct Professor at South Florida Bible College and Theological
Seminary

Somewhere along the way, Western Christianity fully embraced the Greek model of education through lectures and classes, but rejected the Jewish model of learning in community. As a result the Western church is simply not prepared for the end-time revival that is coming before Christ's return. In her book, *Prepare for the Harvest: God's Challenge to the Church Today*, Pamela Christian sounds a warning to the Church that revival is coming and we must change our tactics if we are to be ready for this tidal wave of the Spirit. Christian also provides a sound practical strategy to prepare for this end-time harvest. If you long for this revival and desire for yourself to be fully prepared, I recommend this timely book.

—Dr. Craig von Buseck,
Author, *I Am Cyrus: Harry S. Truman and the Rebirth of Israel*,
manager and editor of Inspiration.org.

This book so appeals to the Christian apologist in me. Pamela Christian's approach perfectly and clearly explains the need for the Church to reach and connect with future generations through spot-on factual and well-researched analysis. The next generation needs and deserves truth and authenticity. *Prepare For the Harvest! God's Challenge to the Church Today* reveals a much needed remedy so the Church can meet people's needs right where they are, while standing firm on God's uncompromising truth. I really loved this book.

—Bob Dutko,

Christian apologist and nationally-syndicated talk-show host

As a premillenialist (of the pre-tribulation variety), I disagree with some of Pamela Christian's eschatology. However, *Prepare for the Harvest!* provides valuable insights concerning the frightening moral state of our culture and how Christians should respond with authentic gospel witness.

—Richard Land, PhD,

President Southern Evangelical Seminary

There is a saying that "The Bible will never comfort you with a lie, it will challenge you with the truth." Pamela Christian's new book: *Prepare for the Harvest! God's Challenge to the Church Today* follows that exact strategy. This book is a roadmap for the reality of our culture today. But it's not just research about our dilemma, it outlines the strategy for a comeback. If you are a coward, this message is not for you. But if you are unafraid to confront the truth of our world and the challenge of transforming it, then this book is for you.

—Phil Cooke, PhD,

Filmmaker, media consultant, and author of
The Way Back: How Christians Blew Our Credibility and How We Get It Back

PREPARE FOR THE HARVEST!

GOD'S CHALLENGE TO THE CHURCH TODAY

Pamela Christian

Math 28:18-20

Prepare for the Harvest!
God's Challenge to the Church Today
Book Five in the Faith to Live By series

Copyright © 2020 Pamela Christian

All rights reserved. No part of this book may be used or reproduced by any means, graphic, electronic, or mechanical, including photocopying, recording, taping or by any information storage retrieval system without the written permission of the publisher except in the case of brief quotations embodied in the critical articles and reviews.

Published by Protocol, Ltd.
info@protocolpublishing.com

Pamela Christian's books may be ordered through the publisher or Ingram Distributors.

Unless otherwise indicated, Scripture quotations are from the ESV® Bible (The Holy Bible, English Standard Version®), copyright © 2001 by Crossway, a publishing ministry of Good News Publishers. Used according to permission. All rights reserved.

Because of the dynamic source of the internet, any web addresses or links contained in this book may have changed since publication and may no longer be valid. The views expressed in this work are solely the views of the author.

ISBN-13: (sc) 978-1732769236
ISBN-13: (hc) 978-1732769281
ISBN-13: (e) 978-1732769243

Library of Congress Control Number: 2019917977
U.S. Copyright Number: 18210082541
Printed in the United States of America.

DEDICATION

In your hearts honor Christ the Lord as holy, always being prepared to make a
defense to anyone who asks you for a reason for the hope that is in you; yet do it
with gentleness and respect.

—1 Peter 3:15

I dedicate this book the family of God—all my contemporary and future brothers and sisters in Christ. May we all realize the glorious gift of salvation and the rich inheritance we have because of God's love and grace. May this understanding be our relentless motivation for becoming workers of His harvest. This book, and the entire book series, is written to help us all better grasp our true identity and authority in Christ, that we may join in lockstep with the Father's plan to bring His will on earth as it is in heaven. Amen.

CONTENTS

ACKNOWLEDGMENTS

It is incredible that there is yet another book in this Faith to Live By series. This book, like the fourth in the series, was inspired and written within thirty days, and that without writing full-time. Clearly, the Holy Spirit downloaded the topic and swiftly guided me in writing the content. All glory and honor is God's.

Given the increase of prophetic words I am seeing about preparing for the Last Days, and the swiftness of writing, I can't help but believe this is an extremely pressing and urgent message for the Church today.

I sincerely appreciate my friends and family who have encouraged me in the process of authoring books. I look forward to the expected personal speaking engagements where I can impart the heart of God revealed to me in writing this series, and I thank in advance those of you who invite me to speak.

I thank those who helped me produce this book, as you are invaluable in helping get God's message out. This includes my endorsers and advance reviewers. Your input, correction, and encouragement are most appreciated.

I greatly appreciate the endorsements I've received for this and all books in the series. I especially appreciate endorsements from leaders of different denominational affiliations acknowledging our differences while focusing on what we hold in common. Unity in the faith does not require uniformity and I believe it is our differences that allow us to reach more people for Christ.

Lee Ann Mancini is a total gift from God and one of the most generous people I have the privilege to know. She is an adjunct professor and board member at South Florida Bible College and Theological Seminary who has not only read all my books in the series, but has invested her time and expertise in reviewing this book with a heart kindred to mine, wanting to help people fully embrace the Christian faith. Lee Ann has helped me seek to fulfill the prophecy spoken over me with her encouragement and support. Especially in light of her extensive education, I am blessed beyond my ability to properly express. I am humbled and profoundly grateful to her.

Lisa Knight is the cover designer for all the books in the Faith to Live By series. Not only is she talented, she partners with the author in wanting to produce excellent book covers and other marketing materials. Her knowledge of the Christian market, as well as the general market, have helped build my brand and have contributed to the various awards the books in the series have received.

Acknowledgment and profound appreciation belong to my husband whose financial support makes it possible for me to serve in full-time ministry. Without God's provision through my husband, the Kingdom work I've contributed to this point in time would not be possible. The lion's share of needed financial resources has been unselfishly supplied by my husband David—seeds he has sown we know God will allow to yield a bountiful harvest.

I cannot end this acknowledgement without expressing my sincere and deep appreciation for my readers and ministry adherents, recognizing Jimmie Hancock, Chaplain, Colonel, USAF Retired, as among my most constant supporters.

The work I do—my life's work—whether through this book series, my television series by the same name, my work in radio, or through speaking and teaching at conferences and retreats—is to be a strong asset to the Church as prophetically spoken over me in 1994. I very much want to help people discover and live in the same life-giving and victorious truth I have been blessed to find. May my ministry in Christ continue to bring benefit to many, with all glory to God.

INTRODUCTION

W riting *Prepare for the Harvest! Confidence in God's End-Time Promises* greatly piqued my awareness of the differing points of view and understanding people have concerning the times in which we live. Listening to various pastors, teachers, and prophetic voices, I hear a lot of excitement about the end-time revival and the unprecedented works of God we will see. What I hear very little about is repentance in preparation for the end-time harvest.

At Jesus' first coming John the Baptist sternly warned the people to prepare the way of the Lord. The word of the Lord came to John, son of Zechariah, consistent with Isaiah 40:3–5. John then went into all the region around the Jordan, proclaiming a baptism of repentance for the forgiveness of sins (Luke 3:2–4). With many exhortations, John the Baptist preached good news to the people—the good news of the coming of the *Messiah,* the Anointed One whom God promised would come to redeem all who place their faith in God's Word—God's promise. Jesus was the Word of God in the flesh—the fulfillment of the promise for a deliverer God made to the first man and woman, Adam and Eve, and to all their offspring.

In these days we live, we are eagerly expecting Jesus' second coming as He promised He would. If a clarion call was needed to exhort people to prepare themselves for Jesus' first coming, how much more important is an adamant alarm for us to prepare for Jesus' return! With Jesus' second coming, God will fulfill His plan to restore humanity and creation, eternally separating the children of God from the children of Satan. These end-time days usher in the last days and the final opportunity for mankind to choose life. The need for people to be informed with truth, the importance of being prepared, and how to make ourselves ready is greater than ever.

I learned of Michael Brodeur and Banning Liebscher's book *Revival Culture: Prepare for the Next Great Awakening* (Chosen Books, 2012) after I completed the manuscript for this book. Imagine the elation I felt learning of their work which provides a witness to the heart of God, confirming my understanding the condition of Christianity in America today.

Research about Christianity in America reveals a decline in the number of people who are genuine born-again believers in Jesus. There is a stupor or a spell that has been effectively preventing people from recognizing truth, causing them to live their lives on the basis of lies. Vast numbers of people are deceived, and because the nature of deception means the victims are unaware of their condition, they continue living on the basis of lies.

The only way deception can be revealed is by an outside force exposing it. This outside force is intended by God to be the Church of all believers, and more so, those called to leadership. Those who are called to shepherd God's sheep are the ones who need to be sounding the alarm, preaching and teaching people to prepare themselves for Jesus' second coming—to be ready before it is too late. This is what I see as God's tremendous challenge to the Church today.

The Church seems to be looking ahead to the glorious days of the anticipated revival, without regard to preparation. Unless we are in the right position, instead of experiencing revival we will experience judgment. We read in 1 Peter 4:17 God's judgment begins with the house of Lord. However, if we intentionally humble ourselves and repent of our unholy ways, we can escape or lessen the judgment and be in position to receive the revival God longs to give.

Scripture expresses the importance for us to humble ourselves; should we fail to do that, we can expect God to humble us. We must be consecrated unto God to see and experience His righteous works. Our focus and efforts must be to be holy and blameless, recognizing the Church is the bride of

Christ who is expected to make herself ready (Rev. 19:7). Our emphasis must be on the full transformation of the heart, with a sincere desire to be wholly surrendered to God through faith in Jesus, by the power of the Holy Spirit. God says we must be holy, because He is holy (1 Peter 1:16).

The Church, especially in America today, is not at all ready. Many people who profess to be Christians are apathetic, complacent, and indifferent regarding many aspects of the Christian faith. There is a commonplace attitude of familiarity with God instead of a proper reverential fear of God. Many Christians do not demonstrate effective faith or the power of God. It is no wonder unbelievers see no reason to become Christians, and worse, have disdain for the Church. There is no doubt evil exists. Unfortunately, evil has found its way into the lives of a great number of Christians in America.

Prophetic voices have been very clear, we are not in a new season—we are in a new era. We are in an entirely new place in God's plan, according to His timeline. God has revealed the keys for His people to abundantly flourish in the days ahead. However, unless we are informed and properly respond, we can personally miss the blessings and therefore suffer the consequences.

This book should also be used as an extension of the fourth book in this Faith to Live By series, identified in the opening sentence of this introduction. This book differs in that instead of providing a general overview of the various end-time doctrinal views, I am challenging the Church to prepare people to be victorious through the great and terrible events that are sure to come.

I believe the Enemy has used deception to cause great numbers of people to believe in a pretribulation rapture—that is when genuine Christians are expected to be taken to heaven before the beginning of the tribulation the Bible predicts. Instead of possessing an informed view about the end times, many Christians have an unfounded "exit-ology" expectation. Highly educated scholars differ about the sequence of end-time events. Technically, we have been in the end times since Christ's ascension. The Bible clearly reveals a continued increase of evil in the world until the return of Christ and His final judgment. Will Christians live through the end times known as the great and terrible tribulation? Reading the book of Revelation indicates there will be Christians coming out of the tribulation. We must be prepared as no man knows the hour or day of Christ's return.

Jesus was moved to compassion when he looked over the crowds of people and declared the harvest is ripe. He therefore implored His followers to pray for workers of the harvest (Matt. 9:37–38). As followers of Jesus, all believers are expected to be workers of the harvest, and to be effective, we need to be prepared. My hopes are for this book to be used by God to confront those who belong to Him, and used by the Holy Spirit to convict Christians to wake up out of their stupor, and make themselves ready before it is too late.

As in the days of Noah, the people who ignored the long-term advance warnings, experienced the time when they were shut out and no longer had the option to repent and be restored to God. So too will there be such a time on earth, according to God's revealed plan. Let us understand the eternal seriousness of our times, repent for ourselves, then in all earnestness help others realize the truth about these last days.

PART ONE

Evaluating the Culture

This know also, that in the last days perilous times shall come.
For men shall be lovers of their own selves, covetous, boasters,
proud, blasphemers, disobedient to parents, unthankful, unholy,
Without natural affection, trucebreakers, false accusers,
incontinent, fierce, despisers of those that are good,
Traitors, heady, highminded, lovers of pleasures more than
lovers of God; Having a form of godliness,
but denying the power thereof.

—2 Timothy 3:1–5

CHAPTER ONE

Understand Revival

A woman nearly thirty years old who had made a wreck of her life by repeatedly making poor choices recalled what little she had learned about Jesus as a small girl. In desperation, knowing she needed help beyond herself, she cried out to God. "God if you are real, and if You can help me, I need You. I need You to turn my life around and make something good of it, because on my own I have proven all I can do is make a mess of it. I realize I have wanted Jesus to be the Savior of my life to prevent me from going to hell. But I have been Lord of my life. If You can help me now, I will not only believe in Jesus as my Savior, I will surrender my whole self to Him as Lord."

In that time of genuine surrender to the Lord, the woman experienced a profound transformation. She heard the voice of God speak to her spirit with kind and loving words of truth about her sin and of His unconditional love for her. She felt God's love, acceptance, and forgiveness extended to her. In that moment, through a proper faith in Jesus and complete surrender, she was personally revived—she was miraculously, spiritually transformed by the power of God's Holy Spirit. And her life has never been the same.

That woman was me.

Some may wonder why we need to be revived, especially in light of the definition. To revive is to restore to life or consciousness, or strength, or energy. As I wrote in the Introduction, most people today live in a stupor—they are deceived and believe what is wrong is right, and what is right is wrong. This reality is foretold several places in Scripture with 2 Timothy 3:1–5 as one such example:

> But understand this, that in the last days there will come times of difficulty. For people will be lovers of self, lovers of money, proud, arrogant, abusive, disobedient to their parents, ungrateful, unholy, heartless, unappeasable, slanderous, without self-control, brutal, not loving good, treacherous, reckless, swollen with conceit, lovers of pleasure rather than lovers of God, having the appearance of godliness, but denying its power. Avoid such people.

I believe both Christians and non-Christians would have to agree our culture has become hostile for all the reasons stated in Scripture. Whether or not a person believes the Bible is relevant, we cannot deny the accuracy of the explanations of the progression of lawlessness and tremendous human discontent.

God made all mankind in His image. In this way we all have a form of godliness. But not all choose to believe the truth of Jesus, preferring instead their own way. Going one's own way is rejecting Jesus and denying God's power that restores our spirit, heals our soul, and sets us free to enjoy the abundant life Jesus died to give us. With great numbers of Americans rejecting Jesus, and those who profess to be Christians failing to have Jesus as Lord, understandably the condition of our culture has been rapidly declining in these days. The condition of people foretold in the Scripture passage above is fulfilled.

Sin is the rejection of God and all that is good. Because the first man, Adam, and first woman, Eve, both rejected God and His ways, the originally created holy spirit within them died. Sin brings death. This means every human being born ever since has been born with the same spiritually dead condition and are at enmity with God. Sin and death are natural conditions we have inherited. Unless a person is revived by God, they remain in this natural, rebellious, and lawless condition. The condition of our culture is evidence of the lack of revival.

Two Types of Revival

Revival is both personal and corporate. Individuals can experience a personal revival that does not impact others on larger scale. My own example of genuinely calling out to God is personal revival. Corporate revival is when many people experience the Holy Spirit convicting them of sin. It's a complete spiritual transformation by a renewal of their hearts through a proper faith in Jesus, by the power of the Holy Spirit. Corporate revival is God intervening in the lives of great numbers of people, demonstrating His power and love in such a way that masses willingly repent—that is they change their mind about preferring their own way and willingly choose Jesus. Revival is a fresh outpouring of God's life-giving Spirit on His people.

Tony Cauchi, publisher of *Revival Library* explains, "Revival is when God reveals Himself in awesome holiness and irresistible power. It is when He visits the world of men to impart a fresh vision of His glory and grace and simultaneously to reveal man's sinfulness, inadequacy and desperate need of God's mercy."[1]

When does God demonstrate Himself in this manner? When people humble themselves, repent, and actively seek Him. We read in 2 Chronicles 7:14, "If my people, *who are called by my name,* will humble themselves and pray and seek my face and turn from their wicked ways, then I will hear from heaven, and I will forgive their sin and will heal their land" (emphasis added).

There has always been a remnant of people who are genuinely surrendered to God, while the majority of people claim to have faith in God, but do not live according to His edicts, preferring instead their own ways. This is no different than the rejection of God by Adam and Eve.

As stated in the Introduction, many people are crying out for the end-time great revival to come. However, I see little being done to prepare for this great and terrible time.

Biblical Revival History

History reveals God provides revival when His people have fallen away from a proper relationship with Him and into sin. When wickedness and evil seem to be overtaking righteousness, even becoming the guiding influence of God's people, the scene is set for God to produce a revival. Therefore, revival includes remedial judgment—corrective judgment upon groups of people. Revival comes upon individuals for a corporate purpose, which goes on to influence other people groups for the greater corporate purposes of God.

Revival is when God intervenes in the lives of His people to reestablish their properly committed relationship to Him, which is entirely for their good. Only when God's people are true to Him do they flourish and enjoy the benefits of all His good promises.

Reading the Old Testament history of God's people, we learn they cycled in and out of relationship with God with what seems to be rapid succession. When wicked kings reigned, the people fell far away from God, which brought judgment upon God's people. When a successor king reigned and recovered godliness, the people experienced a revival and awakening of true worship, albeit only for a season, when another falling away eventually occurred.

In the period of time represented in the New Testament Scriptures, estimated to be some forty years, we see many churches experiencing spiritual setbacks resulting in the need for a revival beginning with judgment.

I hear many Christians calling out for revival, wanting to experience the overwhelming love and power of God, without a proper understanding of what revival will require of them. They are calling forth what they believe will be a benefit without understanding revival includes judgment.

Scriptures reveal there will be a great outpouring of God's Spirit in the last days, generating the last great harvest of souls before Christ's return. With this in mind, I understand the heightened cry for revival. However, we must be prepared for this great revival. This is the stated purpose of this book—for the Church to be prepared for what God is soon to do.

Evaluating our culture today, especially in America, we see a falling away of people from faith in God and from living according to His revealed will. The tremendous increase in lawlessness, the hatred expressed, and the increase of violence are evidences of the diminished influence of Christianity on our culture.

The Pew Research Center on Religion and Public Life published a report in 2015 titled "America's Changing Religious Landscape." It revealed the overall Christian population is declining, although the United States remains home to more Christians than any other country in the world, with seven out of ten people identifying with some branch of the Christian faith. Between 2007 and 2014 the Christian share of the population fell from 78.4 percent to 70.6 percent. More significant, however, is the rapid increase of people claiming no religious affiliation at all, along with increase of those who belong to a non-Christian faith.[2]

More recently, the Pew Research Center on Religion and Public Life survey conducted in 2019 revealed a drop to 65 percent of American adults describe themselves as Christians while those who identify as atheists, agnostics or "nothing in particular," referred to as "nones," stands at 26 percent, up from 17 percent in 2009.[3] Comparing these two surveys it is clear Christianity in America is on a rapid decline.

Considering God's intervention in the lives of His people throughout history, it seems our culture today is ripe for judgment. Since the Church (meaning all who profess Christianity) is commissioned by Jesus to make disciples of all nations, we can expect remedial judgment within the Church.

Modern Day Revival History

Understanding historical revivals helps us prepare for any future revival. Michael Brodeur and Banning Liebscher wrote in their book *Revival Culture: Prepare for the Next Great Awakening* about the lack of preparedness in the Church evident in response to what was known as the "Jesus Movement" of the 1970s:

> For the most part the Body of Christ, the Church, was absolutely unprepared for the new [converts] who were being born again around them. In the early 1970s, only a few churches accepted these long-haired, dirty, braless hippie believers. Most didn't want them soiling their pews or even sitting on their new carpets. Too many traditional churchgoers had no comprehension or value for what God had done by saving a generation. Instead, they looked on with natural, human eyes and failed to behold the sovereign

8

work of the Holy Spirit. Sadly, many of these new believers experienced outright rejection or conditional acceptance. "If you cut your hair and wear a suite like the rest of us," they were told, "then you can be part of our church.

Other churches and leaders who embraced this counterculture harvest reacted in ways that were harmful to these new believers. Some, recognizing the rebellious spirit that was on this generation, instituted a series of teaching and structures that later became known as the Shepherding or Discipleship Movement. New believers were told to submit to their elders and pastors in a way that, in many cases, was abusive and destructive. On the other hand, some groups drifted into cultic beliefs and behaviors and even into licentious practices like those of the Children of God, who used sex and drugs to lure new recruits into their group.

Although many mistakes and failures were committed in response to the Jesus Movement, there was also a strong percentage of leaders who perceived what God was doing and rose to the challenge.[4]

I pray we learn from our past mistakes, else we are in serious danger of repeating them.

Judgment and Revival

Can we experience revival without being first subjected to judgment? It seems many professing Christians believe we can, just as there are many Christians who believe in a pretribulation rapture. But are either of these views what the Bible teaches? Judgment *begins* with the house of God, according to 1 Peter 4:17. Thankfully, God never issues judgment without first providing warning and giving us a chance to repent.

All throughout biblical history, God's main purpose in judging His people has been to get them to return to Him as their only God, requiring they forsake their idols. Idols are anything that supplants God as first and foremost in a person's life.

Gauging the culture of the Church in America, many claim it is idolatrous and adulterous, both conditions repeatedly and harshly judged by God in the Old Testament. God's judgment upon His own people is always to purge us of the sin that we have allowed to enter and participate with. Such is the case of the seven church-cities identified in the first three chapters of the book of Revelation. Only one of the seven church-cities, the faithful church of Philadelphia, received commendation and escaped judgment. All the others were warned of impending judgment if they did not repent. That *all* the people of the other six church-cities repented is extremely unlikely. This seems to be substantiated with the references to God's people living in the end times as found in Revelation 7:13–14:

> Then one of the elders addressed me, saying, "Who are these, clothed in white robes, and from where have they come?" I said to him, "Sir, you know." And he said to me, "These are the ones coming out of the great tribulation. They have washed their robes and made them white in the blood of the Lamb."

I encourage you to read with all sobriety the first three chapters of the book of Revelation because they serve as a warning to the Church today. Anyone who belongs to God through faith in Jesus, who has forsaken a proper faith relationship with God without repenting, will be judged by God. Scriptures are clear God disciplines His own first. We bring judgment upon ourselves by the choices we make. God will deal with His own first, then with those who do not belong to Him.

Instead of realizing we will be judged if we do not repent, the Church in America ignorantly cries out for revival without being prepared. We need to heed the warnings of Scripture if we want to avert judgment. As God's people we are instructed to be holy—meaning set apart from the world and wholly aligned with God and His ways. Increasing numbers of Christians believe they are in right standing with God—that God is pleased with them, no matter what they do or what they believe. The increase of alternative lifestyles, sexual sins, lust, love of money, divisive doctrine, and so much more are increasing because professing Christians are not elevating the standard of holiness. Many Christians are deceived in their understanding of God's grace, are not living righteous lives, and are active sympathizers, if not participants, with ungodly behavior. With history as our guide, it seems clear God revives His people first through judgment, then according to the degree of repentance in response to His advance warnings.

God administers judgment upon nations, churches, and individuals to awaken us and lead us to turn away from sin and toward Him. This type of judgment is known as *remedial judgment*, as opposed to *final judgment*. When final judgment occurs it is too late for repentance. God's remedial judgement is intended to bring us to a repentance that leads to life. Remedial judgment is rendered to get our attention, stop our downward cycle of sin, and bring us back to God.

The Pretribulation Rapture Theory

In both ancient times and New Testament times (the era in which we live) a remnant of faithful believers call out to God on behalf of the whole nation (Old Testament) and the whole Church (New Testament). Again in the book of Revelation only the faithful church-city of Philadelphia was commended and rewarded. All seven of the church-cities represent the Church of believers, yet only one church-city was told they would escape the hour of trial that is coming upon the whole world to try those who dwell on the earth (Rev. 3:10). If this escape is representative of a pretribulation rapture, then clearly only a small remnant of Christians will escape the end-time tribulation. At least portions, if not all of the remaining church-cities will be upon the earth during the great and terrible end times.

Who wouldn't want to believe in a pretribulation rapture that allows us to escape the worst times the earth will ever see? No one wants to sign up for suffering. The pretribulation rapture doctrine, more fully treated in the fourth book of my Faith to Live By series, is the newest of all end-time doctrines. It was popularized by Hal Lindsey with his book *The Late Great Planet Earth*, and the *Left Behind* book series by Tim LeHaye and Jerry B. Jenkins. The Bible, however, makes it clear only some Christians will escape, and I understand it to be those who are holy, represented by the Philadelphia church-city in Revelation. During the last days, when God is judging the people on the earth, many more will repent and find their eternal destiny in heaven. However, some will refuse to place their faith in Jesus; and this willful choice will find them spending eternity in hell.

We have to understand how serious the times are in which we live. Our choices today determine our eternal destiny. Living ungodly lives, which originates in our hearts, separates us from God and all that is good, even if we are born-again believers. The liberal cultural mindset today deems what was once considered sin by God to be no longer sinful. This is a lie from the pit of hell that many Christians have accepted as truth. What God declared sinful is for all time sinful. God is very clear; His people must be holy because He is holy. God cannot tolerate sin and He has given us the means to refuse to participate with sin. When we succumb to sin as His own we should expect to experience discipline in the form of remedial judgment.

Perpetuating the doctrine that the whole Church will be caught up in a pretribulation rapture, in my considered opinion, is a scheme of the Enemy to deceive Christians and to prevent us from being prepared. We must begin teaching with great urgency the need to repent and cooperate with God to get His truth deep in our hearts. We will then live godly lives and be an influence upon the people of this earth to choose eternal life through faith in Christ. When Christ returns He will administer final judgment on both the living and the dead and there will be no further opportunity to repent.

Intercession and Repentance

In addition to repentance, intercession is a key element to revival. Intercession is prayer that is offered on behalf of others. Intercessory prayer in our days should include asking the Lord to help people everywhere realize their sin, and turn to God in repentance through faith in Jesus Christ.

We read in 2 Chronicles 7:13–14:

> When I shut up the heavens so that there is no rain, or command the locust to devour the land, or send pestilence among my people, if my people who are called by my name humble themselves, and pray and seek my face and turn from their wicked ways, then I will hear from heaven and will forgive their sin and heal their land.

In the Bible, rain is considered blessing, whereas devouring locusts and pestilences are considered judgment. God's grace and desire is for us to repent of our own accord, sparing us from remedial judgment, and restoring

13

us to right relationship with Him. We can and must be in earnest intercessory prayer for the Church and our nations. Our intercessory prayers can usher in repentance before judgment, making the judgment lighter or averted altogether.

Al Whittinghill explains more from the book of Isaiah:

> In the days of Isaiah the people of God were languishing because they had turned from the reality of authentic intimacy with God. They were perplexed by the ongoing "difficulties" and lack of blessing that their carnality had caused. They came to Isaiah and asked him to inquire of the Lord why things were not getting better. God spoke a word to Isaiah that he gave to the people. We would do well to mediate on it. God desires to show mercy and spoke verse 16 to them stating that He was "astonished" that there was no intercessor. He repeats this in Isaiah 63:5. Authentic intercession and effectual prayer by God's people is what God has chosen and is waiting for to put in "the scales of justice" and stop imminent judgment when His holiness demands it![5]

There are many examples in Scripture where intercessory prayer brought relief from judgment. While intercessory prayer might occur under other circumstances, the Old Testament prayers of the servants of the Lord on behalf of others were most often given to avert the divine wrath that was imminent or had already begun.

Rick Carmichael offers additional insight to the importance of intercessory prayer:

> God's activity is that He sends judgment upon the land because of the sin of His people. If, and when, this happens God calls His

14

people to fully respond to Him by humbling themselves, praising, seeking His face [prayer] and repenting of sin so that forgiveness and healing can come. You may very well be feeling more of the grief and burden of seeing the breakdown in your culture and in the lives of those around you, perhaps even in your own life.

If you sense the increasing judgment of God in your nation or in the lives of those around you, instead of giving up all hope as lost, realize that your full response to the Lord can help divert greater judgment and bring the spiritual awakening that is desperately needed.

As you and I pray for the Lord to awaken the Church and the lost, we can pray with great faith and expectation. There is no doubt that the Lord wants the Church to come to life and for many lost people to yet be saved before Christ returns. He does not want any "to perish but for all to come to repentance" (2 Pet. 3:9) and for "all men to be saved and to come to the knowledge of the truth" (1 Tim. 2:4). The Lord has sent revivals in the past that have impacted nations, and He has on His heart to do it again in our day, not because anyone deserves it (we deserve the opposite), but because of His great compassion and concern for the eternal well-being of all people.[6]

Birthing Revival

As we pray for the Lord to awaken the Church and the lost to the realities of sin in our midst, we must pray with great faith and expectation. We have many promises in Scripture that say if we pray anything according to God's will, He hears and answers our prayers. Is it the will of God for His people to repent of sin and be restored? Absolutely! Therefore, let us pray from a confident stance, assured our prayers are right and pleasing to God. God would far rather we humble ourselves than for Him to have to humble us. Intercessory prayer from victory without fear of defeat is essential to usher in the right conditions for revival. Not only does God want to send revival, He is seeking us as intercessors to help usher revival in.

What will we experience when revival comes? John Piper explains it this way:

> In the history of the church, the term revival in its most biblical sense has meant a sovereign work of God in which the whole region of many churches, many Christians has been lifted out of spiritual indifference and worldliness into conviction of sin, earnest desires for more of Christ and his word, boldness in witness, purity of life, lots of conversions, joyful worship, renewed commitment to missions. You feel God has moved here. And basically revival, then, is God doing among many Christians at the same time or in the same region, usually, what he is doing all the time in individual Christian's lives as people get saved and individually renewed around the world.[7]

In a true revival, we can expect many glorious experiences. We have explored the first two realities which are intercessory prayer and repentance. Another mark of true revival is the overwhelming desire to exalt Jesus more than anything else, even above oneself. Henry Blackaby, founder of Blackaby Ministries International and an influential evangelical pastor said:

> Powerful preaching is a hallmark of true revival. Revival preachers demonstrate their commitment to the authority and sufficiency of the Scriptures, with bold, urgent, and uncompromising preaching,

as they set before God's people the way of life and death. Powerful, Spirit-filled sermons concerning sin, Christ, and the cross penetrate the hearts of the saved and lost alike with the realities of eternity.[8]

As Paul Chappell writes, "There is no revival without making Christ preeminent and His Word primary."[9]

Hearts that have been revived will provide evidence that Jesus is priority in their lives by not only speaking of Him but being obedient to His ways. People will willingly volunteer to help with God's kingdom work on earth, knowing being involved in God's plans for this world, according to our God-given spiritual gifts and natural talents, is the highest calling. Love and compassion for our fellow man will be evident and sharing the gospel message will be the primary demonstration of Christ's love.

In prior revivals, which will be explored in Chapter Twelve, the changed hearts of people aligned with God and His ways resulted in many cultural reforms moving out of perversions of various sorts and into righteous living. Social injustices and abuses are dealt with, corruption is exposed and corrected—not by imposition of law, but by hearts willingly repenting and laying down ungodly behavior and striving to increase in God's ways.

Ellen White says:

> A revival of true godliness among us is the greatest and most urgent of all our needs. To seek this should be our first work. . . . But it is our work, by confession, humiliation, repentance, and earnest prayer, to fulfill the conditions upon which God has promised to grant us His blessing. A revival need be expected only in answer to prayer.[10]

17

The Bible is clear; in the last days all manner evil and wickedness will increase. We certainly have been experiencing that in our time. However, God's plan includes for righteousness to also increase and outpace the increase of evil. I believe we are at an important juncture in God's time-line where the Church is being called out concerning our apathy and even downright disobedience to God and His ways.

Personal and Corporate Reflection

We need both personal and corporate revival today in a tremendous way. As will be revealed in the next chapter, even though we desperately need both personal and corporate revival, we are far from understanding we do. Many professing Christians and churches are simply going through the motions of faith without their heart being fully engaged. God is an all or nothing God. When God the Father gave His Son on the cross to die for the sins of the whole world, He was all-in. When Jesus willingly gave up His deity to take on human form, to be the only suitable sacrifice for those will receive Him by faith, He was all-in. When the Holy Spirit bodily raised Jesus up from the dead by His power, He was all-in. When people of the early church learned all that Jesus said and did by faith, they were all-in, knowing their faith in Christ put their very lives at risk. That is being all-in.

If we want more of God, then we must give Him more of us. I heard a pastor ask a congregation, "Are you committed to Jesus?" He paused as people considered their response then said, "I hope not. Because if you are committed to Jesus you are still in charge. However, if you are surrendered to Him, He is in charge." I say we need both—we need to be fully committed in order to be fully surrendered.

In the next chapter, we will examine cultural realities similar to looking in a mirror to more accurately see ourselves for who we are as individual Christians and the Church in America.

CHAPTER TWO

Identify Cultural Realities

The Church has been a cornerstone of American life for centuries, but much has changed in the last thirty years. While there are some vital churches in America, overall the view of unbelievers that the Church is dying seems to be deserved.

These realities are researched and objectively determined by Barna Research Group's "The State of the Church 2016." The report states:

> Millennials in particular are coming of age at a time of great skepticism and cynicism toward institutions—particularly the church. Add to this the broader secularizing trend in American culture, and a growing antagonism toward faith claims, and these are uncertain times for the U.S. church.[1]

What about you, do you personally identify with the Barna Group's findings? Do you agree the Church in America is experiencing uncertain times? I definitely do, evidenced by my desire to help prepare the Church for the days ahead.

I wrote the first book in this Faith to Live By series, titled *Examine Your Faith! Finding Truth in a World of Lies*, out of a reaction of shock, outrage, and heartbreak in response to an article published by ABC News, "Americans Surprisingly Flexible about Religion and Faith." The article explains Americans are creating their own religious faith by selecting from various established religions and creating a religion of their own preference. An article by the Pew Forum on religion and public life says:

> Nearly six in 10 Americans from all religions blend their faith with New Age and Eastern beliefs, like astrology, reincarnation and the spiritual—not just physical—benefits of yoga. "What we're really finding here that we haven't known before is how much Americans mix and match their religious beliefs and practices. This is, how often people who are regular churchgoers also believe in things like astrology and reincarnation," said Alan Cooperman of the Pew Forum. "Individual Americans hold within themselves elements of diverse religious traditions. And they practice in many cases, more than one faith."[2]

The research further found 49 percent of those polled report having a religious or mystical experience . . . a spiritual awakening, which was up from 22 percent in 1962. Additionally, 29 percent of Americans say they have felt in touch with someone who died—that is up from 18 percent in 1996.

This report concerns me greatly as it indicates people are misguided regarding the realities of the spiritual world. The highly successful Harry Potter series is just one example of how popular entertainment has influenced our culture to unknowingly dabble in matters of witchcraft and the occult. The Bible is clear God's people are to remain far separated from witchcraft and the occult, and only be involved with the spiritual realities of

God and His Kingdom. However, it seems the Enemy of God has been quite successful in deceiving people, intriguing them with spiritual realities that are evil in origin. Many partner with the Enemy, unaware. The woeful ignorance of our culture is perpetuated by people simply accepting what they are taught, without personally researching for themselves. Cultural ignorance about matters of religious faith was the driving force behind my writing *Examine Your Faith! Finding Truth in a World of Lies.*

Culture of Deception

Reaching the culture with the truth is a difficult challenge. People do not knowingly choose to base their worldview and belief systems on lies. Therefore they believe they have based their life on truth, which may not be the case. This is why I emphatically state, unless we examine what we believe and why we believe it, we can easily be deceived and not know we are deceived.

Culturally, we have shifted from a literal interpretation of Scripture to a subjective interpretation. Considering many believe truth is relative, this shift is to be expected. However, I see this as a tactic of the Enemy of God, who is another reality many Americans deny.

In another report by Barna Research Group, people were asked if they thought "Satan is a living being, or is a symbol of evil." Of those Christians polled, 40 percent believe "Satan is not real, but a symbol of evil," with an additional 19 percent saying they somewhat agreed with the statement. A minority of Christians (26 percent) indicated they strongly believe Satan is real by disagreeing with the statement, while 9 percent agreed Satan is real somewhat. In the same report we learn most Christians do not believe the Holy Spirit is a living force. Overall, 38 percent strongly agreed and 20 percent agreed somewhat that the Holy Spirit is "a symbol of God's power or presence but is not a living entity."[3]

The basic tenets of the Christian faith have been systematically demolished with increasing numbers of people being led astray. No one wants to live their life on the basis of lies, yet many people actually do. The essential basic tenets of the Christian faith are critical for those who want to possess truth. If the Bible's clear explanation about the existence of Satan and hell can be ignored preferring instead one's own ideals, then the entire Bible is under personal and subjective scrutiny.

Those who do not believe in the existence of Satan are unable to discern his presence. Satan is the father of all lies who has influenced people to conclude he does not exist so he can continue to increase evil without any opposition. He has influenced many people into wrong beliefs as part of his scheme to dethrone God. Satan has no problem discrediting himself and making Christ's followers ignore his existence and causing Christians to consider the Holy Spirit simply a symbol of God's power and presence, and not a living entity.[4] Of course! Think about it: if people do not believe in a literal Satan who is subject to the power and authority of the literal Holy Spirit, then they are powerless against His schemes, unable to call on the literal Holy Spirit who has the power to defeat the literal Satan. They are deceived by Satan and therefore victims of Satan whose only purpose is to deceive and destroy anything of God's.

Statistics Are People

There are inconsistencies evident in the Barna research, because people have not fully thought through their "truth claims." Barna recognizes and comments on these inconsistencies. These are far more than boring lists of statistics and opinions. We need to realize these are precious people for whom Christ died who are being deceived and who are unaware of their condition. Christian leadership and Christians who know the truth must stop assuming people have their life solidly based on biblical truth, and adamantly preach and teach the Word of God correctly. People will never repent from a reality if they are unaware of it.

Tolerance, relativism, political correctness, avoid offending others are all tactics of the Enemy to prevent the Church from taking and expanding its rightful place of authority against evil. The weakened state of Christians in America is cause for both judgment and revival. However, if enough Christians recognize the urgency of these days, repent, intercede, and boldly take a stand teaching and preaching the truth in love, people can become aware of their condition and repent, lessening the situational judgment.

Religious Pluralism

The Pew Forum on Religion and Public Life article also reveals how increasing numbers of people believe all religious roads lead to the same God and same heaven. This belief is known as *religious pluralism*. Religious pluralism is an emotional or subjective conclusion without sufficient research of objective, verifiable evidence to support the claim. Attempts to blend religions and philosophies by taking the tenets of different faiths to create a faith of one's own preference actually makes the individual "god" of their own life.

With all this in mind, what we in fact have are rapidly increasing numbers of people genuinely seeking spiritual truth who are woefully deceived. Even the matter of truth itself has been altered with many people claiming truth is personal and relative. Adherents of *relativism* seek to be tolerant and accepting of the beliefs of others, believing that is a loving thing to do. Yet what good is love that allows a person to live their life on the basis of deceit?

25

Additional People Facts to Consider

It is estimated there are 80 million millennials in the U.S. Studies reveal 70 percent of millennials raised in the Church disengaged from it in their twenties, with one-third Americans under thirty now claiming "no religion."[5] Over half of millennials with a Christian background (59 percent) have at some point dropped out of going to church after having gone regularly, and half have been significantly frustrated by their faith.[6] Peter Boatwright, co-director of the Integrated Innovation Institute stated, "Millennials are widely believed to have less faith in God and are less active in religion than their parents and grandparents."[7]

I would like to add to Boatwright's findings. It is not just the millennials who are rejecting Christianity. The falling away from Christian ideals, values, and morals can also be attributed to the baby boomers with their radical departure from organized religion, western ideologies, and conservative morals. What had been known as sin by generations before baby boomers was not only challenged but rejected in the 1960s.

A positive reality about millennials is their reputation for being passionate about causes. Millennials have been deemed the social justice generation.

Claims that millennials elevate physical needs over spiritual needs and forgo evangelism altogether is inaccurate according to the Barna Research Group. Despite the Pew reports of Christianity being on the decline, Barna's research indicates this is not the case among millennials.

Rob Hoskins, president of OneHope wrote an article citing:

> While the evangelistic practices of all other generations have either declined or remained static in the past few years, Millennials are the only generation among whom evangelism is significantly on

the rise. Their faith-sharing practices have escalated from 56% in 2010 to 65% in 2013.

Not only that, but born again Millennials share their faith more than any other generation today. Nearly two-thirds (65%) have presented the Gospel to another within the past year, in contrast to the national average of about half (52%) of born again Christians.[8]

Hoskins asked millennials to evaluate the statistics about their generation and respond to the perception that their generation has *laissez-faire* faith. While more than a handful responded with sentiment such as "I agree" or "It is sad but true," it stirred up quite a bit of passion. The comments from some of the respondents follow:

I completely agree, and I think it is perhaps one of the most dangerous attitudes one can have in relation to faith. Research still indicates that this generation is very spiritual; the problem is that the spirituality is ill-defined, immature, and no longer explicitly Christian. In many ways, this generation is the generation of apathetic deism. We still believe in a transcendent god, just not enough to care about how that belief impacts the way we think, behave, and interact with others.

Jesse Daniel Stone

It breaks my heart because I know it is often true. I believe in the Western, consumeristic, entertainment-driven "Christian" subculture, my generation has not been confronted with their need for God, the reality of their sin, and the cost of following Christ. The version of Christianity they are familiar with is something that would cause anyone to have laissez-faire faith—a watered-down, feel-good moralism that is dictated more by culture than by God's Word. God's Word is radical. God's Word is deep. God's Word is authentic. We are jaded. We are deaf. We are asleep. This generation, I believe, if authentically encountered with the confronting Truth of Scripture would have a much different kind of faith.

Diandra Bree Hoskins

My generation is one of paradox. We embrace a laissez-faire approach to many elements of this world, while being more strict, passionate, or opinionated about others. Though statistics may show a laissez-faire approach to the Christian faith, the reality is that underneath the statistics, this generation may be the most passionate, opinionated, and inspirational generation yet—it's just that our "faith" has been co-opted by post-modernity and hyper-individualism. MTD (moralistic therapeutic deism) is a more accurate description of our faith, whether we are "Christian" or not.

Ryan Secrest

It's a stereotype, but one not without merit. If churches preach that membership doesn't matter, that doctrine divides, and that Christianity is primarily about feeling good and doing the right thing, we shouldn't be surprised when individuals find other communities and other doctrines that make them feel better and seem to be doing better things. At the same time, research indicates that church involvement (not necessarily "evangelical" identification) remains steady. Many Millennials are exploring the deep and wide of the Christian tradition, and experiencing faith in profound and sustaining ways."

Brandon Ratliff[9]

While some other comments disagreed with the label of millennials being laissez-faire about their faith, for the purpose of this book, we need to have a genuine understanding about the people we want to reach and serve. I deeply appreciate these well-articulated statements allowing us to determine greatly improved ways to connect with this generation.

Another blog article titled "Let's Stop Pretending Christianity is Actually Relevant, Okay?" by Benjamin Sledge states: "A recent Barna survey reports only 18% of Millennials find Christianity relevant to their lives. That is not surprising if we are honest." The author cites the Christian push back against Supreme Court decisions regarding same-sex marriage, removal of Christian symbols, and Scripture in public places, and such. He makes the point that Christians are unaware of how much of the culture they have already lost. Yet Christians expect the culture to uphold their values. He writes:

> It's a strange practice to ask people who don't hold the same beliefs as you to conform to your morals because you quoted a book they don't read. My friends that aren't Christians have never tried to force their morality on me, so this is an odd practice in Christendom. Even Jesus didn't blame pagans for acting like pagans. Yet, many Christians insist their beliefs apply to the culture at large even though most don't share the same beliefs.
>
> What we need to face is that public perception has shifted. We live in post-Christian America where we're no longer relevant to the culture at large. Whatever influence Christians used to have, much like a parasite trying to reconnect to its host for fear of

dying, many Christians are thrashing about trying to create waves and convince people they are relevant within our culture. But sadly, instead of men and women looking like Jesus we sure have a lot of talking heads. We sure have a healthy dose of condemnation in our ranks. We love being "right" instead of the hard task of humility.

Is it any wonder we're not relevant?[10]

What Sociologists Understand

Culture is understood to be our collective, common values and beliefs, language, communication, and shared practices among a group of people. Culture consists of knowledge, common sense, assumptions, and expectations, and includes rules, norms, laws, and morals that govern society. Culture is important for shaping relationships, maintaining and challenging social order, determining how we make sense of the world and our place in it, and shaping our everyday actions and experiences in society. Culture is also what we do, how we behave, how we perform, how we walk, sit, carry our bodies, and interact with others. Culture influences how we respond in different situations, how we express identities of race, class, gender, and sexuality. "Culture also includes the collective practices we participate in, such as religious ceremonies, the celebration of secular holidays, and attending sporting events.[11]

> Culture is important to sociologists because it plays a significant and important role in the production of social order. The social order refers to the stability of a society based on the collective agreement to rules and norms that allow us to cooperate, function as a society, and live together (ideally) in peace and harmony.[12]

The Church Culture

The church culture, like other cultures, is one of the most important concepts in sociology because it plays a crucial role in social lives. However, unlike other cultures, the church culture is expected by God to impact and attract people from all other cultures.

The values, beliefs, morals, communication, and practices that Christians share in common provide us with a shared sense of purpose and a valuable collective identity. French sociologist Émile Durkheim says, "When people come together to participate in rituals, they reaffirm the culture they hold in common, and in doing so, strengthen the social ties that bind them together."[13]

Culture is a force that can be used for oppression and domination, or for creativity, resistance and liberation. "Without culture," says Nickie Lisa Cole, "we would not have relationships or society." The role the Christian Church is to have on culture can produce the best possible outcomes for all involved. However, the Church has failed society and even its own members. Identifying and owning our failures is essential to bring about reformation, which we will explore in Chapter Five.

Biblical Illiteracy

G. Shane Morris in his article about biblical illiteracy wrote, "Writing in the *Washington Post*, Christine Emba admits many Americans—particularly those in news media—are more likely to recognize a "Harry Potter" reference than a biblical one. This is a problem because "as a reference point, the Bible is a skeleton key that unlocks hundreds of years of culture, from Shakespeare to Khinde Wiley." Morris continues,

31

But the cost of not knowing the Bible goes deeper still—past Shakespeare . . . Magna Carta and the Civil Rights movement. Ignorance of Christianity undermines the deepest aspirations of the Western mind, and our ability to know why we have these aspirations. Our longing for freedom, for exodus, for a promised land, for equality between sexes, and races, classes—for dignity, compassion, and decency to our fellow man, no matter his home country—our very convictions on the universality of our Constitution's claims about freedom and "inalienable rights"— these are the parts of us conformed to the contours of Christianity. The thing in us that cries out when we see a stranger's toddler washed ashore on a Turkish beach or causes us to cheer when a firefighter rushes back into a burning high-rise to save one more soul—that is the bit of us shaped by the Bible.

The only ignorance worse than not knowing the book that made us who we are as a civilization is believing we can go on being civilized without that book. The marks of the Bible upon the West and its people are deep. Very deep. Like the color of the cut flower, they linger long after they're severed from their source of nourishment. But they are not indelible. We were barbarians before the God of the Bible found us. And we can become barbarians again.[14]

Morris writes about the danger of Americans not knowing the Bible, and he is entirely correct. However, what about Christians not knowing the Bible? How can the Church impact society if we do not know our own document of religious authority?

Study after study in the last quarter-century indicate American Christians increasingly do not read their Bibles; neither do they engage their Bibles or know their Bibles. It has been said we are living in a post-biblically literate culture. We claim we believe the Bible is the Word of God—His divinely inspired, inerrant Word. Yet Ed Stetzer, Ph.D, [Billy Graham Distinguished Chair of Church, Mission, and Evangelism Executive Director, Billy Graham Center at Wheaton College] former executive director of Nashville LifeWay Research, an evangelical research firm specializing in research on church and culture reports only 45 percent of those who regularly attend church read the Bible more than once a week. Over 40 percent of the people attending church read their Bibles occasionally—maybe once or twice a month, if that. And worse, 18 percent of churchgoers claim they never read the Bible.[15]

I have heard the average American—Christian or not—owns at least three Bibles. True or not, those who do not have one in their home can read it on the internet. Biblical illiteracy is not lack of access. It is lack of reverence. It is lack of belief or doubt regarding the importance of the Bible. The popular view about the Bible is that it is an important piece of literature as opposed to the living, transforming Word of God.

Impact of Biblical Illiteracy on Society

In 1962, the Bible was taken out of our public school system by our government, sending a message to society that human intellect is superior to divine revelation. It was also the start of the demise of the Church's influence within society and culture. Today, nearly six decades later, we are experiencing the grave impact as a result.

Education expert William Jeynes, professor at California State College in Long Beach and senior fellow at the Witherspoon Institute in Princeton, New Jersey explained there is a correlation between the decline of U.S. public schools and the U.S. Supreme Courts 1962 and 1963 decisions that school sponsored Bible reading was unconstitutional. Since 1963 Jeynes said there have been five negative developments as a result of the court's decision:

- Academic achievement has plummeted, including SAT scores
- Increased rate of out-of-wedlock births
- Increase in illegal drug use
- Increase in juvenile crime
- Deterioration of school behavior.

School behavior problems reported by teachers from disrespect for class and campus rules to rape, robbery, assault, burglary, and arson have steadily increased from 1963 to the present.

Jeynes provide additional insights:

> So we need to realize that these actions do have consequences. When we remove that moral fiber—that moral emphasis—this is what can result. Now the question is, given that there is a movement to put the Bible as literature back in the public schools and a moment of silence and so forth, can we recapture the moral fiber—the foundation that used to exist among many of our youth?[16]

The movement to teach Bible as literature, rather than as the powerful Word of God gives me no hope that such a study will restore what we have lost. As a nation we have lost respect for authority, law and order, and the due process of law. As a culture we have lost civility, integrity, and honor. Many of our American rights are slipping away: religious freedom, freedom of speech, and the right to bear arms are just three examples. We have also lost the proper value of human life, the value of marriage and family, and

God's moral values. As individuals we have lost hope. This is but a small representation of all we have actually lost.

For these reasons, the Church needs to lead the way in engaging people with correct biblical doctrine while living out the Word in real-life situations, which will be discussed in Chapter Twelve.

This chapter is not exhaustive, but it provides a good starting point for understanding our culture and the Church.

In the next chapter we will explore the perception about Christians common in our culture today.

CHAPTER THREE

Cultural Perceptions About Christianity

To assist in the effort of educating our culture to gain wisdom and understanding in addressing real-world needs, it is important to take a critical look at the image and reputation of the Church.

Jonathan Bock and Phil Cooke, coauthored *The Way Back: How Christians Blew Our Credibility and How to Get it Back* (Worthy Books, February 2018). They concluded non-Christians view Christians and the Church as judgmental, negative, and phony. Bock and Cooke wanted to understand why Christians and the Church are viewed this way. They established four identifying markers: church attendance, prayer, Bible study, and tithing. Then they gathered research from the most reliable companies and concluded the non-Christian view of Christians and the Church is a correct assessment.

In a television interview with host Jeanne Dennis, Bock said 70 to 80 percent of Americans self-identify as Christians, depending which research is used,. (This range is greater than more recent studies.) However, of that group, only 20 percent attend church weekly. The percentage of Christians who believe prayer is essential to their faith is 63 percent. Specific to Bible reading, 40 percent *of those regularly attending church* reported they rarely or never read their Bibles. Regarding tithing, less than 10 percent actually observe this discipline. Bock's interview regarding his research was conducted before the most recent Pew Research Center on Religion and Public Life survey conducted in 2019.

In Bock's words, "We're dictating to others what we don't do. We've become like the fat guy at the gym, lecturing others what to do for good health. Working out is hard. Wearing yoga pants is easy, and we have a lot of Christians out there that are proving they are just wearing yoga pants. They're not doing the hard work. The first issue is we've got to get back to work. We've got to get back in shape."

In short, he is saying we have got to walk the talk.

Instead of Church leaders teaching about holiness, obedience, devotion, sanctification, and other disciplines essential for a vibrant and visible faith, they are creating an experience when they should be making disciples. Americans are attending church less, praying less, reading their Bibles less and giving less of their time, talent, and funds.

In seeking to understand the status and reputation of Christianity in American society, we need to ask, "What is happening?" and "What should be done?"

Considering Both the Positive and Negative

Glenn Stanton, a leader with Focus on the Family, and Rick Richardson, a leader with the Billy Graham Center, provide timely insight with each of their recently published books. Both make extensive use of survey findings and other data, and both take a myth-busting approach to the misconceptions about American Christianity. It seems, in general, Christians overreact to negative news about their faith, while at the same time do not properly respond on the positive findings.

Rick Richardson and Ed Stetzer coauthored, *You Found Me: New Research on How Unchurched Nones, Millennials, and Irreligious Are Surprisingly Open to Christian Faith,* (IVP Books, June 18, 2019). They examined the survey commissioned by the Billy Graham Center in 2016 polling 2,000 Americans who are classified as "unchurched." This survey asked these people how they perceive Christians and Christianity, asked about their willingness to talk about matters of faith with Christians, how they might respond if invited to a church meeting, and which types of invitations they would be most willing to accept. This is surprising, especially in light of Barna's findings provided in Chapter Two.

Richardson's and Stetzer's take-away is many unchurched Americans have a respect for Christians and are open to being engaged in discussions about faith. The authors reveal 42 percent of the unchurched think Christianity is good for society, 33 percent admire their Christian friends' faith, and up to 67 percent indicated they would be willing to attend certain types of church events. The authors conclude, among the unchurched are "a massive number of people who are open to being invited, persuaded, and connected to a local congregation." The author's findings encourage us to realize not all unchurched are hostile to Christianity. Any concern of rejection should therefore be allayed allowing us to comfortably and lovingly share our faith.

According to a LifeWay *Facts & Trends* article, 82 percent of the unchurched are likely to attend church if a friend, co-worker, neighbor or family member invites them. We need to understand that is eight out of ten people! The LifeWay article included Gallup estimates that 43 percent of Americans—135 million people—are unchurched. If the research is even close to accurate, the implications are staggering. More than 110 million people would attend church if they were invited.[1] What constitutes an acceptable invitation will be discussed in Chapter Twelve.

The Gospel Coalition, U.S. edition, suggests the decline of Protestantism may be good news for Christians. In 2013 half of all Americans identified a Protestant. However a survey by *ABC News/The Washington Post* in 2018 finds just a little more than one in three claim to be a Protestant Christian. Among all Protestants, a little more than half (56 percent) claim they are evangelical or born again. This number has remained steady since 2003.

Additionally, the survey found the largest shift to be among the "none" category. This group saw a 16 percent increase among young adults (age 18– 29) and political liberals. Among this group 35 percent are religiously unaffiliated, compared to 13 percent among those age 50 and older. The percentage of nones is also higher among men than women (25 percent vs. 17 percent). Additionally, the survey found that 35 percent of liberals report no religious affiliation, compared with 21 percent of moderates, and 12 percent of conservatives. About one in four Democrats (23 percent) and independents (25 percent) do not report having a religion, compared to just one in ten (10 percent) for Republicans.[2]

Interpreting the Evidence

Joe Carter, author of *Why the Decline of Protestantism May Be Good News for Christians*, said in interpreting the data, "What this means is not that America has become 'post-Christian' but rather that society is now in a 'post-pretend-Christian' state. If we take the opportunity to be the church, we may find that America is not post-Christian, but is instead maybe 'pre-Christian.' It may be that this land is filled with people who, though often Christ-haunted, have never known the power of the Gospel."[3] At least, I will add, not yet.

The increase of the nones and the decline in Protestantism may actually be a good thing, if we see it as clearing the way for us to provide these precious people a right understanding of the gospel and the nature and will of God.

Further Considerations

People have witnessed the Church, government, politics, and education fail society. People have experienced the failure of marriage and family, the increase of violence, the disrespect for law, order, and authority. People have been taught humans evolved from an explosion in the cosmos, meaning we come from nothing and we will end with nothing. Life, therefore, has no significant meaning or purpose. The result is the increasing unrest and a highly contentious culture.

Yet, the Pew research reveals people are seeking to find meaning and purpose and to lay hold of something greater than themselves. The stark increase of people seeking spiritual or mystical experiences is evidence of supreme dissatisfaction with powerless religion. It is evidence of an intrinsic belief that there must be something more.

Millennials provide encouraging evidence of people's hunger for truth, their desire to be mentored, and to be part of an effort that is greater than themselves. Barna Research Group indicates the millennials to be the most idealistic generation in many generations. They want a place to fit in and make their own significant contributions in keeping with their goals for social justice. They have passion and an altruistic outlook. They see the Church as irrelevant and phony for a variety of reasons. Painting with a broad brush but accurate brush they see:

- The Church is judgmental.
- The Church is not clearly distinct from the world.

- The Church is not comfortable with people outside the Church culture.
- The Church is internally focused.
- The Church is not making a cultural difference in this world today.
- The Church is not united but rather competitive to a fault.
- The Church is not forthcoming in welcoming, training, and equipping others for leadership.
- The Church is ineffective in helping people with real life issues.
- The Church does not have making of disciples as a priority.
- The Church is not engaged in the culture.
- The Church is subject to the government by the 501(c)(3) status.
- The Church promises much and delivers little.
- The Church remains silent concerning godly principles needed for us to flourish in every mountain of society: religion, family, education, business, arts/entertainment, media, and government.

While millennials and other people groups see the Church as stated above, in truth there are churches whose members follow biblically-based doctrine and make tremendously positive contributions to society and culture. Unfortunately, human nature often causes us to conclude on the whole, instead of recognizing where blame is actually warranted. This means the Church as a whole needs to take ownership of our reputation and turn it around so we can be effective in the work God has called us to do.

My first paid published article was titled "Since God Ordained Civil Government, Why Aren't Christians Involved?" It is my considered opinion the Church in general has withdrawn from society and culture, succumbing to fear, which is of the Enemy. Fear is a tool of the Enemy that renders faith impotent; this is why I believe the Church is largely ineffective today.

Various people groups recognize this and want nothing to do with the Church. At the same time, they partner with independent ministry organizations to create a platform for dynamic contributions of truth and righteousness that the world desperately needs.

The Next Generation

Among the millennials who have found Christ and are born again, there is great hope for the Church to become effective workers of the harvest in these last days.

The generation after the millennials is referred to as Generation Z or Gen Z. A landmark study from Biola and Talbot alumni, along with the Barna Research Group, offers key findings about the next generation. In an article, Octavio Esqueda writes:

> You've heard all about millennials. But what about the generation coming right behind them? Gen Z, born between 1999 and 2015, is beginning to reach college and high school, and in many ways, they're vastly different from their millennial predecessors—less religious, more success-oriented, more diverse, more captivated by technology and more likely to embrace different views on sexual identity. Is your church prepared to help them flourish in this new cultural landscape?
>
> Gen Z were born in a context where religion in general, and Christianity in particular, are no longer a major influence in American culture. The secularization of society has been a trend in the last few years, especially in the Western world, and Gen Z are growing up in this new social context. In fact, according to the

Barna study, teens 13 to 18 are twice as likely as adults to say they are atheist.

Gen Z tends to be inclusive to all people, practices and perspectives. They are open-minded and sensitive to other people's feelings and opinions. On the positive side, they embrace divergent perspectives and are more inclusive than previous generations. They are comfortable with people who are different than them and tend to be less judgmental because of those differences. On the negative side, they tend to be wary of declaring that some actions are morally wrong or simply incorrect. They seem to have a flexible moral compass that leads them to unclear paths and prevents them from making decisions or judgments according to solid values and convictions.[4]

Interpreting Trends

We need to understand what the trend away from Christianity means. The *Gospel Coalition*, U.S. edition, explains:

In 1971, only 5 percent of Americans claimed no religious affiliation. In fact, until 1993 the nones never composed more than 8 percent of the population. But something has changed to cause a rapid increase in the abandonment of religion.

"The growing ranks of religiously unaffiliated Americans have been fed by striking simultaneous losses among white Christian groups," says Robert P. Jones, PRRI CEO and author of *The End of White Christian America*. "The religiously unaffiliated now outnumber Catholics, white mainline Protestants, and white evangelical Protestants, and their growth has been a key factor in the transformation of the country over the last decade from a majority white Christian nation to a minority white Christian nation."

What are we to make of this decline? Perhaps we should rejoice.

"The big trends are clear," Ed Stetzer said in 2015, "the nominals are becoming the nones, yet the convictional are remaining committed."

This decline of nominal Protestantism may be good news if we see it as an opportunity to share the Good News with those who didn't realize what they abandoned.[5]

According to a *Religion News Service* opinion article, "Where is Christianity Headed? The View from 2019," the growth in American Christian denominations is driven mostly by nonwhites, whether Catholic or Protestant, evangelical or mainline. Over the past half-century, 71 percent of growth in Catholicism has come from its Hispanic community. In the Assemblies of God, one of the few U.S. denominations to show overall growth, white membership slightly declined while nonwhite membership increased by 43 percent over 10 years. Multiracial congregations are expanding, drawing one in five churchgoing Americans, and these churches report a higher level of spiritual vitality compared to racially homogeneous congregations.

The trends for Christian churches outside America are overwhelmingly glorious:

> Globally, Christianity is recentering its footprint and becoming a
> non-Western religion. For 400 years, the faith has been molded by
> the largely European culture that came out of the Enlightenment.

But today its vitality is coming from emerging expressions of Christianity in Africa as well as in Asia and Latin America.

As the yearning for authentic spiritual experience moves from the head to the heart in this new environment, Spirit-filled communities are flourishing. Today, one of four Christians in the world identifies as Pentecostal or charismatic, with Pentecostalism growing at roughly four times the rate of the world's population itself.

The popular image of Pentecostals as television preachers extolling a prosperity Gospel and flitting around on private jets obscures the real causes for much of the movement's explosive growth: small Pentecostal communities among the marginalized in the Global South that are providing empowerment and social transformation.[6]

Experiencing the authentic power of faith in Christ is likely the draw for the Pentecostal and charismatic churches that are growing four times the rate of the world's populations itself. Today one in four Christians worldwide identify as Pentecostal or charismatic.

It is clearly stated in 2 Corinthians 4:20, "For the kingdom of God does not consist in talk but in power." Based on several Scriptures, I believe strongly that in these last days we will see greater demonstrations of the power of the Holy Spirit. I think this is the evidence of the Holy Spirit that the world of skeptics, nones, and others are hungry for.

The Church has remained divided about supernatural gifts being available today. Based on my research, this division will be allayed as we move closer to Christ's second coming. It is not God who wants us to be deceived, but the Enemy. I pray for those who believe the supernatural gifts are not available today to reconsider their conclusion. The following question, which

I have asked others in the past, has been a catalyst to reconsider this belief: "Why would God tell us of the great and terrible events of the last days, and not equip us to be able to overcome?"

I believe the supernatural gifts have always been available. I believe the Enemy of God is the one who wreaks havoc on our proper knowledge of truth. We will not wield what we do not believe, so the Enemy gets the upper hand by weakening the Church.

The Cry of the Culture Today

In my research, it is clear that the non-Christians, especially the millennials, are big fans of Jesus but not so much of His followers and the churches where they worship. Generation Z is even less enthusiastic about Christianity. Authentic conversation, authentic faith that transforms, true hope and help, are what people everywhere desire.

Pastor/author Dan Kimball shares how he took time to step outside the busyness of ministry and listen to some college students from what was known to be one of the more anti-Christian campuses in California.

> It was these "pagan" students who gave me such incredible hope for the Church. I was leading a young adults' ministry we had recently started at the church I was on staff with at the time, and occasionally during worship gatherings, we showed man-on-the-street video interviews to set up the sermon. For an upcoming message series on evangelism, we decided to go to this college campus to interview students and hear firsthand their thoughts about Christianity. We asked two questions: "What do you think of when you hear the name 'Jesus'?" and "What do you think of when you hear the word 'Christian'?"

47

When they answered the first question, the students smiled and their eyes lit up. We heard comments of admiration such as, "Jesus is beautiful," "He is a wise man, like a shaman or a guru," "He came to liberate women." One girl even said, "He was enlightened. I'm on my way to becoming Christian."

What an incredible experience! These students on the very campus I kept hearing was so "pagan" talked about Jesus with great passion. However, when we asked the second question, the mood shifted. We heard things like, "Christians and the Church have messed things up," and "The Church took the teachings of Jesus and turned them into dogmatic rules." One guy said, "Christians don't apply the message of love that Jesus gave," then jokingly added, "They all should be taken out back and shot."

Now, I realize you could quickly dismiss these comments— "They may like some things about Jesus, but they obviously don't know about His judgment and teaching on sin and repentance." That may be true, but what's important, and so haunting, is that these students were so open to Jesus. Yet, they didn't at all like what they have equated and understood to be "Church" and "Christianity." They definitely liked Jesus, but they did not like the Church.[7]

Reflecting upon the students' answers, Kimball explains only two of sixteen students interviewed personally knew someone who was Christian. Based on that, he understood their impressions of the Church and church leadership came from what they saw in the media or from the more aggressive street evangelists. Without a relationship with a Christian, they had no reference.

One question we must ask is, *Are we personally involved with, or actively seeking to have relationship with non-believers?* Sure, we all have acquaintances who are non-believers, but do we have a sufficient relationship with these acquaintances to begin talking about our faith? We need to seriously consider developing friendships that will allow us to share the gospel out of love for these friends.

As Kimball noted, we are so used to staying in our Christian "community" that we have become isolated in our own subculture. While we might expect objections to the Church to include, "The Church is only after your money," or "The sermons are irrelevant," Kimble provides the six most common objections among those twenty to thirty years old:

1. The Church is an organized religion with a political agenda.
2. The Church is judgmental.
3. The Church is dominated by males and oppresses females.
4. The Church is homophobic.
5. The Church arrogantly claims all other religions are wrong.
6. The Church is full of fundamentalists who take the Bible literally.

We need to thoroughly explore all objections we hear from people, with loving hearts and persuasive words. How we can provide remedies for these and other objections is the focus of Chapter Six.

In the next chapter we will consider the common human needs and how the Christian Church is best suited for helping to satisfy these needs.

CHAPTER FOUR

RECOGNIZE HUMAN NEEDS

God made mankind in His image to be His children and to enjoy relationship with Him. This is our highest calling. Even though each natural born human since Adam and Eve is born estranged from God because of sin, we still have an innate desire to know God. Until we actually know Him, we may not be aware this innate desire is for God. It simply feels like a deep-seated lack—a personal desire and a sense of unfulfillment not fully understood.

Sin estranges us from God and all that is good. Sin is a naturally-born condition we have inherited. It is not what God ever wanted for us. Being estranged from God is the consequence of the first man and first woman rejecting God and His ways, preferring themselves and their own ways instead. However, because of God's great love for us, He provided a way each individual can escape the ravages of sin that results in eternal death. He promised the first man, Adam, and first woman, Eve, a Deliverer or Redeemer who would redeem those who choose life by placing their faith in God and His promises.

God is three persons in one: God the Father, God the Son, and God the Holy Spirit. Each is co-equal in power and authority. Yet each operates from a different position.

The historical person, Jesus the Christ or Anointed One, was God's Word in the flesh. Jesus was the personification of God's promised Redeemer. Jesus, the Son of God, the Second Person in the triune Godhead, willingly took on human form. Although he was both fully God and fully human, He set aside His deity to live solely in His humanity. In His humanity, He lived a sinless life, making Him the only suitable sacrifice to atone for the sins of the world. He was severely beaten and scourged, then crucified for our sins. Three days after His death, however, Jesus was miraculously resurrected by the power of the Holy Spirit, the Third Person in the Godhead. He lives! Jesus lives, and anyone who places their faith in Jesus as their personal Savior from sin, will escape eternal damnation and instead receive eternal life with God in heaven. Being reunited with God is a gift from God, by His grace and love. There is nothing we have done to deserve His love. He will never stop loving and desiring an intimate relationship with us.

Finding God the Father and First Person of the Godhead, through placing our faith in Jesus, by the power of the Holy Spirit, is the only way our deep-seated unfulfillment will ever be satisfied. This explains why those who have not placed their faith in Jesus are still searching and live restlessly. God wants all who belong to Him to find Him, so He has placed the desire deep within us to help drive us to discover Him.

The Church has the responsibility of helping people of all nations find God through faith in Christ. It is my prayer this book will be a source of encouragement for the people of the Church to become fully engaged as workers of the harvest. Knowing God, and living our lives for Him, allowing Him to transform us, and doing His will to bring His Kingdom on earth as it is in heaven, is the highest calling we can have. It is what the world of unbelievers are spiritually starving for. In Chapter Six we will explore ways we can better be about our Father's business.

The Innate Desire to Belong

In addition to a longing to know God, ingrained into every human being is the desire to belong—to be loved. When we are loved, we are esteemed and valued. And when we are confident we are loved and valued, we move forward in life aware of our significance, believing in our ability to make a positive difference in this world.

While the above description is true for everyone, it seems younger generations are more frustrated in these areas than older generations. We explored some of the reasons why in the previous chapter. So now let us further consider deep-seated unfulfilled desires to allow us to have proper empathy and compassion, and know how to reach out to help people satisfy their basic human needs.

I believe Abraham Maslow's Hierarchy of Needs, a theory in psychology proposed in his 1943 paper, "A Theory of Human Motivation" published in *Psychological Review*, is quite good. His theory is comprised of a five-tier model of human needs, often depicted in the shape of a pyramid. Maslow's study was on learning what motivates people. His theories parallel many other theories of human-development psychology. Moving from the base of the pyramid to the top, the terms for the five discoveries Maslow observed are, "physiological," "safety," "belongingness and love," "esteem," and "self-actualization."[1]

If Maslow's theory is correct, then we all desire to belong and be loved, to be esteemed, and to enjoy the realization or fulfillment of our talents and potentialities (self-actualization). I do not see these desires being satisfied in even the slightest degree with the belief that all creation has come from a cosmic event followed by evolution and the survival of the fittest. If all of creation, including humanity, is the result of a random explosion, then there is no basis for virtues such as heroism, selflessness, human kindness, or morality of any kind; there is no origin for any expression of love.

Roy Baumeister and Mark Leary argue:

> Belongingness is such a fundamental human motivation that we feel severe consequences of not belonging. If it wasn't so fundamental, then lack of belonging wouldn't have such dire consequences on us. This desire is so universal that the need to belong is found across all cultures and different types of people.[2]

Believing Before Belonging

In many ways, the Church model needs to be rebuilt to better reach people with the truth of God's Word. We cannot expect people to come to a church they have problems with to explore a faith they have not seen appreciably demonstrated. Finding ways to get outside our four church walls and into the community is essential. It is also far more consistent with Jesus' instructions to His disciples to "Go therefore and make disciples of all nations, baptizing them in the name of the Father and of the Son and of the Holy Spirit, teaching them to observe all that I have commanded you. And behold, I am with you always, to the end of the age" (Matt. 28:19–20).

The Church seems exclusive to outsiders for a few misunderstood reasons. Actually, Christianity is open to anyone who wants to belong. We need to better communicates that Jesus made it clear there is no other way to be rightly related to God, except by faith in Him. God the Father will not force people to come to faith in Christ. It must be a decision of the will for each individual. Therefore, contrary to claims by some, Christianity is excusive; it is entirely inclusive for anyone who wants to place their faith in Jesus.

Churches that want people to believe in Jesus before they can enjoy belonging in a local church community are making it difficult for people to learn what they could be part of. I certainly wouldn't agree to belong to anything before knowing more about it. I hope this book inspires churches to make adjustments and be more intentional about holding outreach events.

Additionally, churches need to establish procedures to welcome unbelievers, including and discipling them so they understand what it is to be a Christian, and to enjoy the Christian experience. When an unbeliever has been welcomed, and discipled, and makes the decision to receive and believe in Jesus as their personal Savior, there should be celebration with all church members invited. Perhaps this celebration would incorporate the new believer's public baptism. Or a simple announcement could be made that another person has come to the Christian faith. This allows the congregation to rejoice, affirms everyone, and celebrates Jesus.

Consider how your church operates today and where it might be missing the mark. Pray and seek the Lord to reveal new and creative ways the church can better reach the lost for Christ, especially during this end-time harvest season.

The Church as a Place of Healing

The Church is to be a hospital, open to all who want to come to find the healing they need. In preparation for the end-time harvest, we have a great deal that needs to be restructured:

- We need to restructure our separatist point of view.

- We need to increase discernment of those who are genuinely seeking from those who are not.
- We need to extend ourselves to those open to the gospel .
- We need to strategically engage people.
- We need to know and teach the essentials of the Christian faith.
- We need to know how to lead a person to Christ.
- We need to have a strategic discipleship program in place.

The often-labeled "Seeker Friendly Movement" opened the doors of the church with programs and enticements to draw unchurched people. I believe the movement caused confusion by preaching a politically correct and watered-down version of the Christian gospel so not to offend. Presently there is discussion within the Church about "Belonging Before Believing." The premise is to welcome people and satisfy their human need to belong, before they are converted.

A better idea is found in the Bible. It is what Jesus described in John 13—a community that profoundly believes the gospel, so its life is notably marked by love for one another, demonstrated by carrying one another's burdens, praying for one another, sharing in practical ways with those in need, expressing joy and hope, all because of faith in Jesus. Such a community, Jesus said, will provoke those on the outside not only to recognize they are on the outside, but generate a desire to come in.

Michael Lawrence, senior pastor of Hinson Baptist Church in Portland, Oregon expresses it this way:

> The image that comes to mind is of a bakery on a cold, snowy day. Whiffs of delicious bread and hot chocolate occasionally waft outside. And a child has his nose pressed against the window pane. That glass is a barrier. Without it, the warmth and delicious smells

would soon disperse in the cold wind, and no one would know there was anything good to be found there. But it's a transparent barrier, allowing that child to see the good things inside and invite him in. And there is a way in, a narrow door that he must walk through. Until he does, he can see and appreciate what's inside, but it's not his to enjoy. Once he walks through, it's his for the asking.[3]

Lawrence continues, "When non-Christians encounter your church it should be like standing at that window, not staring blankly at a brick wall."

We want to do all we can to demonstrate it is better where we are, without any hint of arrogance, but only loving enticement. We want to have a visible depth of genuine relationships in our congregations that cause the visitor to see people caring for one another and going out of their way to serve one another. They should hear biblically-sound preaching that addresses genuine human needs, and experience truly joy-filled worship in song and prayer. Since more things are "caught than taught," the specific church community needs to be led into what it is to truly be the Church.

Lawrence sums it up beautifully:

> So go out of your way to create a community that welcomes the outsider. Give thought to the language you use. Be deliberate in your hospitality. And be strategic in your transparency. Like a bakery that pumps the delicious smell of its bread outside, publicly celebrate the stories of grace and transformation that are happening in your midst. And then, when you've done all else, make the Gspel clear and invite people to respond to it in repentance and faith. Call them, not to walk an aisle, but to enter

through the narrow door, and join with you in the riches of faith
in the Gospel.[4]

In Chapter Six I provide some practical steps we can take to better accomplish the Church Jesus desires.

Welcome Those Not Like You

We have adages such as "Birds of a feather flock together" because of the truth they represent. As the Church, however, our goal must be to share the gospel with all people. This is easier said than done because of our human nature of categorizing everything. Our desire to be part of the "in crowd" naturally and unfortunately creates an "out crowd." Cliques and sub-groups are everywhere and generally have harmful side effects. Church leadership can bring unity to the body by being aware of cliques and encouraging members not to form them.

In the last days' harvest, we are going to see great numbers of people come to Jesus from every walk of life. The Church must be prepared not only to welcome them but disciple them. It is true Jesus invites us to come just as we are, but He does not intend us to remain in the same condition. A strategic discipleship program set in place before the revival begins is paramount.

I host an internet television program on HSBN.tv and other networks, named after my book series, Faith to Live By. My stated purpose for the programs I produce is to discuss topics that are common to most people, either directly or indirectly, that are not discussed in the majority of churches. I had the privilege of interviewing Walt Heyer, a man who was born male who underwent numerous procedures and processes to become a female, only to be tortured by his choices and desire for Jesus. His story of all he experienced in his journey, including narrowly escaping suicide, is heart wrenching.

However, I was most impressed with the church's response in finally being receptive to Walt. Even while Walt was outwardly Laura, they could see his torment and genuine desire to be set free, and offered non-judgmental help. Pastor Farrar shared the following in Walt's book concerning what he and his leadership team grappled with:

> The issues facing us weren't really about Laura/Walt, they were really about what kind of church we were. I believe the Spirit was inviting us into a new level of obedience and trust. I had some sense that how we dealt with Laura/Walt would determine the type of leaders and the type of church we would be. We had talked (even bragged) about being a community of grace, yet here was a person whose need forced us to either live that out in the midst of uncertainty and trust, or choose safety and pass Laura/Walt by. Our call was to obey the Lord in ministry and not preserve the status quo or avoid criticism.[5]

How would your church respond to a person who was a man going by the name of Walt who showed up the next week as a woman by the name of Laura? Pastor Farrar said pastors and elders are right to be concerned about protecting church members. He added, "It's a small step from proper concern for the good of the church to protecting our reputation as leaders and avoiding criticism." It is clear from Jesus' example that His character was defamed due to His commit to loving needy, even "scary" people. Luke 7:34 is an excellent example of how Jesus was criticized.

During my interview with Walt he shared how he found it especially moving when he learned Pastor Farrar and his board discussed how some people might leave the church when they saw him attending. But they concluded if some did they probably needed to leave the church and find a place that would better suit them.

During the interview Walt said:

> I was clearly broken and hurting before the Lord, not rebellious or defiant. They realized this, which meant I was one in whom they should invest.
>
> While my past choices were, by my own admission, at best foolish and destructive, I'm longing to honor God in the midst of my pain, and my willingness to follow the truth was apparent. I was crushed and bowed before God seeking His will in the midst of the mess my life had become.

The beauty of Pastor Farrar and the church embracing Walt is what made all the difference in Walt's life, allowing him to enjoy the freedom and victory Christ achieved for all who come to Him.[6] Walt ultimately married one of the precious women from Pastor Farrar's church and together they minister to others with sex change regrets—a tremendous example of the great harvest that comes from sowing seeds.

Revival Will Reveal Who We Truly Are

One version of an adage from the 1950s is "Christians are like tea bags. You find out what they are made of by putting them in hot water." Imagine the soul-searching Pastor Farrar and his board underwent being presented with a precious human in need who was very different from their other church members. Pastor Farrar mentioned they did not have the training or experience or any other frame of reference except the example of Jesus.

With this last days revival we will witness various people coming to Jesus, seeking the local church to help disciple and guide them. Churches need to be prepared to help:

- People with substance addiction
- People with pornography addiction
- People from dysfunctional families
- People from criminal lifestyles
- People suffering domestic violence
- People in serious financial condition
- People who are homeless.

Jesus always forewarns us so we can be prepared. Just as John the Baptist urged the people to prepare the way, I am sounding the alarm. Repent and be organized and prepared because the Kingdom of God is at hand.

In the next chapter we move into evaluating the Church. We will consider the Church's corporate and individual failures and what must be done to institute remedies and avenues for success.

PART TWO

EVALUATING THE CHURCH

But if we judged ourselves truly, we would not be judged. But
when we are judged by the Lord, we are disciplined so that we
may not be condemned along with the world.

—1 Corinthians 11:31–32

CHAPTER FIVE

Church Failures and Follies

The Church is rightly held to a higher standard. The Church of all believers is to be holy, just as our God is holy (1 Pet. 1:16). Not everyone properly understands the biblical definition of the word *holy*—it is quite different from our standard dictionary definitions.

The Old Testament Hebrew word for holy is *qodesh* which means being apart, set apart, separated, sacred, others focused, transcendent, and totally other. Holy has the idea of heaviness or weight of God's glory. In the New Testament the word for holy is *hagios*, which means set apart, reverent, sacred, and worthy of veneration. As God's children, we are to reflect the character, will, and nature of our holy God.

It is sad that most of us can think of at least one church leader who made the headline news because of a sinful decision. In some cases restoration occurred over time. However, I am unaware of a restored church leader who achieved the same level of success before his indiscretion. We can also recall headlines about different ministries that were scrutinized for excessive financial personal gain.

All Christians, not just church leadership, live in the proverbial fish bowl on display for others to view. Most people have empathy for a person who unintentionally falls and fails. However when a person's sin or failure is a willful choice, it is quite another matter. Just as we are more strict with our children when they disobey in an area they definitely know is wrong, God deals more strictly with willful sin. God disciplines those He loves for their good, just as parents do with their children. When we know better but still sin, we set ourselves up for more strict discipline.

Sin Never Impacts Just One Person

When I was teacher for an independent, interdenominational Bible study, we had classes for children and classes for women. Children were welcome from infants up to early teens. We held our classes in a host church. The leadership graciously allowed us to use their facilities so we took extra care of the church building. However, one day the toilet system in the men's rest room became completely clogged. It had to be one of our boys that caused the issue since the plumbing worked the first few hours of our being there.

A boy about nine years old approached me with his mother, his head hanging in shame. He admitted he was the culprit, and his actions were intentional. He apologized through tears, then left, clearly distraught.

The next week when we met for classes, the boy's father showed up to apologize. He explained he had disciplined his son and had told him, "Sin never impacts just one person." At the time I registered the reality of his statement, and the phrase has helped me display compassion in the years since.

When sin such as affairs, abuse, or fraud occur, especially by high-profile church leadership, countless lives are devastated and faith is often shattered. Church members and family members associated with a fallen church leader are devastated sometimes beyond repair. Because of this type of behavior those who are unchurched find another reason to reject the Church entirely.

Carey Nieuwhof, pastor, podcaster, and author of *Didn't See it Coming: Overcoming the Seven Greatest Challenges that No One Expects and Everyone Experiences* blogged:

> Remember, for every mega-church pastor who has exited, there are probably 10 or maybe 100 smaller church pastors whose congregation and families are just as devastated. Only their stories never make the headlines.
>
> I'm not casting stones. But I am writing so that all of us who lead anything (big or small) can look inside and notice the warning signs before it's too late. Before yet another church loses its leader. Before yet another countless thousand people wince and say, "I told you so" or "Yeah . . . figures" and the collective eye roll/anger wave gets unleashed once again and more people walk away from Jesus.
>
> Because, believe it or not, I think failure is in all of us. And yes, I think the seeds of failure are in me too. None of us are exempt. But if you know what to look for . . . if you know where the danger lies, maybe, just maybe, you can finish well. Because not only are the seeds of failure in all of us, so are the seeds of finishing well.[1]

I encourage you to read the entire article. However, for the purposes of this book, I will simply list the pitfalls Nieuwhof identifies as reasons given by the church leaders who fell.

1. It just got bigger than I could handle.
2. I created a world where nobody challenged me.

3. I stayed too long.

4. Somewhere along the way, I lost my soul.

5. I invested too little time at home.

As Nieuwhof stated, there are many long-time Christian leaders who no doubt finished well. Billy Graham was certainly one of them. Christian leaders or individuals are wise to follow what has been called "The Billy Graham Rule," and what became known as the Modesto Manifesto.[2]

Below is a summary of the four-point guideline with my summary statements below in italics.

- Financial Integrity—Graham and his team would not raise money themselves at crusades.
  Intentionally remain unaware of who gives what to avoid any favoritism.
- Sexual Integrity—they wouldn't fall victim to affairs or impropriety.
  Never meet alone with a member of the opposite sex.
- Respect for Local Churches—Graham and his team built up local churches rather than compete with them.
  Church unity fails in an atmosphere of competition.
- A Commitment to Accuracy in Reporting—Graham and his team would not exaggerate how many people attended or how "successful" the ministry was.
  God exalts the humble.

I strongly believe in establishing and maintaining personal accountability with a group of respected, mature Christians who are not going to be yes-men or yes-women. With a proper accountability we can reduce the power abuses that seriously harm countless numbers of people, and deal with matters according to proper church discipline. Any Christian, leader or individual, who is unwilling to be under a system of accountability should be suspect. Church leadership needs to educate and disciple on the topic of accountability.

Failure to Recognize Cultural Opportunities

My own personal view is the cultural and social problems we experience today in the United States are in part a result of the September 11, 2001 series of four coordinated terrorist attacks by the Islamic terrorist group al-Qaeda. That was the day average citizens were made aware how serious the conflict between American and Middle Eastern religious and political philosophies and ideals had become. In my considered opinion, the shock of the attacks, and the terror and fear that fell upon many Americans brought confusion and distrust that has continued to escalate to the present day.

That unfathomable experience left people all over the world with questions, including:

- Where is the protection of the government?
- What might happen next?
- How do we recover?
- What safeguards can we put in place?
- Where is God in all this?

The Church had a tremendous opportunity to demonstrate where true and certain hope is found. Immediately after the attacks local churches were filled to capacity for what ultimately lasted three, maybe four weeks. *Sociological Spectrum* published Jeremy E. Uecker's article, "Religious and

Spiritual Responses to 9/11: Evidence from the Add Health Study" which stated:

> The terrorist attacks of September 11, 2001, are without question the defining moment of the 21st century to date. In the wake of this national tragedy, many people exhibited renewed religious commitment. According to Gallup polls, religious attendance the first weekend after the attacks was up six percent from the weekend before (Walsh 2002). Religious pundits proclaimed the last months of 2001 to be a time of unprecedented religious and spiritual revival in the United States. But not everyone bought into this appraisal of the situation. Indeed, by November polls were already indicating that church attendance had retreated back to normal levels. Despite the immensity of the attacks and the considerable amount of public discourse regarding their religious and spiritual implications for Americans, however, these simple church attendance figures are the basis for much of our social scientific knowledge about Americans' religious and spiritual responses to 9/11.[3]

Christian churches in the United States had a tremendous opportunity to demonstrate the power, authority, and truth of Jesus, to provide instruction about the anti-Christ spirit, and win genuine converts to Christ. However, noting the short-lived surge in church attendance, what people encountered was powerless, irrelevant religion that offered no compelling reason to recognize the Church as the source for finding personal and national victory.

Since the purpose of this book is to learn what we need to know in order to disciple the great numbers of people expected in the last days' harvest of souls, let us place the lesson of 9/11 at the top of our list.

Fear in the Church

In my years teaching for the independent, interdenominational Bible study, I recall being utterly dumbfounded at the noticeable attitude of pastors protecting what they considered their personal territory.

As our classes met in host church facilities, there were times we were asked to find another place, when the church we had been meeting in had the need to use the building or rooms on the day we met. This was not an easy task, but it was mine to do.

I would contact pastors from other churches, explain that the Bible study is an independent, interdenominational, parachurch organization. Sometimes that was the end of the conversation. Understand, however, the organization is worldwide, has been operating since 1975, and still functions wonderfully today. The Bible study commentaries are written by various theologians from seminaries and also pastors, representing mainstream traditional Christian instruction. Then an editorial team reviews and edits the commentary making sure it is wholly aligned with Scripture, and creates the weekly study questions and written commentary. It is an amazing organization that offers deep four-way inductive study materials. Because it is interdenominational, the Bible study has strict rules to follow to always show respect for differing doctrines and make certain to stay centered on correct biblical doctrine that we all hold in common.

However, I was repeatedly met with resistance by pastors who wanted to guard their flock. I understand the importance of pastors protecting their people. However, what I experienced smacked of protection at the expense of unity.

Other pastors who spent more time learning about the Bible study expressed concerns about our class taking away from their efforts, citing that their own Bible study would suffer if ours was offered. To that I recall thinking, *What in the world? How can we have too many Bible studies? Our class meets during the day on Thursday, which might actually be better for those who can't attend the church's class.* Still others plainly expressed they were concerned they would lose members of their congregation to our class.

When I first needed to seek a new facility for our class, I thought the most difficult aspect was feeling like I was asking for a handout. Although the organization's classes do provide a small portion of the class donations in appreciation to the host church, it was nothing like what it would be if we rented. Instead, what turned out to be the most difficult was seeking to overcome the objections many had, all based in fear of the loss of attendance and finances.

The interesting reality is most churches that host these Bible study classes actually experience increase in their church membership. But unless they were willing to reconsider their objections, we were subject to their created territorial distinctions. Where is the unity in this?

The Bible instructs us to establish and maintain unity. This does not mean we blur the lines of denominational distinctions. The book of Revelation lists seven different church-cities, clearly indicating God recognizes we will congregate with differences or distinction. However, distinctions are not to create division. And based on my experiences, the division from these pastors was rooted in fear. Fear is the tool of the Enemy to demolish faith.

In my years in ministry, I have experienced other examples of fear-based divisions that are either of a competitive or independent spirit in nature. When Christian leaders maintain a subtle but obvious spirit of competition, wanting to somehow outperform other area churches, there is no atmosphere of unity. When Christian leaders maintain a distant and independent attitude, there is no highway for unity. Isn't pride at the root of competition and independence? There is so much to be said for linking arms and sharing resources, serving one another with our gifts, talents, and abilities. Instead, we often see church leadership rejecting new perspectives at the expense of a greater good.

Following the example of the early church we should want to share and uplift any genuine, biblically-sound Christian ministry. The attitude that parachurch organizations are a threat to churches is unfounded, more often than not. The Bible study I taught for and the Billy Graham Evangelistic Associations are two excellent examples where parachurch ministries actually support and build up local churches. Given the impending great end-time harvest, and the sheer increase in numbers of people who will be knocking on church doors, I am convinced: "Working together we can accomplish much more," which is the moto of my speaker's bureau *Exceptional Keynote Speakers*. We refer to the bureau as EKS.

I and my new EKS partner have established a roster of seasoned Christian men and women with a wide variety of gifts and talents from different denominations and from all across the United States. We come alongside churches and Christian organizations to help them plan and produce community events to attract the unchurched. By partnering with existing Bible-based Christian organizations, we are taking the gospel outside the four church walls to reach the lost for Christ.

Departure from Early Church Model

Christianity's beginnings was that of a small sub-sect of the Jewish faith. At the time, Rome ruled the world and pagan practices were the norm. Most of the civilized world worshiped Greek gods. Drunkenness, festivals, and temple worship with prostitutes were the norm.

The Church today is also seeking to function in a secular culture. I am quoting again from Sledge's blog post to understand the culture for the early church disciples:

Many Christians found themselves persecuted and tortured [by the Roman culture] for their strange beliefs and due to the fact they welcomed slaves, treated women as equals, and demanded husbands treat their wives with respect and fidelity. Church funds were used to buy the emancipation of Christian slaves. When Roman fathers would leave unwanted children in fields to die, Christians would adopt the children and defy the social structure by caring for them. [Christians] lived counter-cultural and showed love, grace, and affection towards those with different beliefs. This perhaps became most evident when multiple plagues struck Rome in 165 AD and later from 251 to 266 AD.

At the height of what became known as the Plague of Cyprian it was estimated some 5,000 people a day were dying in Rome. Many Romans fled the city believing it the anger of the gods. Most nobles, doctors, statesmen, and priests fled the city in hordes leaving the poor to suffer.

Instead of fear and self-preservation, Christians quickly invaded the city and cared for the poor, sick, and dying at great risk to their own lives. What they understood was simple: God loved humanity, and so to love God back, one was supposed to love and care for others just as Jesus did. During this time period, Christians not only buried their own, but also pagans who had died without proper funds for burial. Reports estimate some churches fed 3,000 people daily. Once the plague hit Alexandria, the Christians there risked their lives performing simple deeds of washing the sick, offering food and water, and consoling the dying. Rome tried to even emulate this model, but it failed because for Christians it was done out of love, not duty. Romans began to marvel and often whispered in the streets "look how they love one another. [4]

Not surprisingly, Christianity rapidly expanded.

The description from the early church is not at all consistent with the realities of the Church in America today. While I am aware there are some individuals and perhaps some churches in America following the model of the early church, generally we are not known by Christ's love.

Feeding Carnality

The Seeker Friendly movement, in my opinion, largely contributed to the confusion about Christianity that exists today. The traditional teaching regarding the standards and characteristics Christians are to acquire were overlooked to not offend anyone and to get more people into the church. While it is true we can come to God just as we are, transformation takes place when we place our faith in Christ. Our spirit within us is regenerated into a spirit that never before existed. From this point we are to cooperate the Holy Spirit to be transformed more and more; this is known as sanctification. Sadly, because the watered-down doctrines that have been taught and adopted by many in church leadership, we have many "carnal Christians." These are people who may be born again, but the standards of the Christian faith do not govern their daily lives. Their life focus is all about seeking what satisfies themselves, instead of tending to the needs of others, which is a core value of orthodox Christianity.

Benjamin Sledge wrote another article titled "Let's Stop Pretending Christianity Is Even 'Christian' Anymore." He says, "The vast majority of

Christians can't even explain the main tenet of their faith and look very little like their founder. Why?" He calls it "The Cult of Feel Good Deism:"

> Sociologists Christian Smith and Melinda Lundquist Denton coined the term "Moralistic Therapeutic Deism" after interviews with 3,000 teenagers. What they discovered is that many of today's youth view religion and Christianity under the following set of core beliefs:

1. God wants people to be nice and fair to one another.

2. The central goal of life is to be happy and to feel good about oneself.

3. God doesn't need to be involved in your life, unless something is going wrong and you need it resolved.

4. Good people go to heaven when they die.

Most adults ascribe to this view of moral and therapeutic deism as well. God is a cosmic genie or butler who gives you Werther's Original candies—much like your WW II vet grandad did—as long as you're nice.

Orthodox Christian beliefs thus become whatever makes you feel good or makes you happy. When I say "orthodox" I don't mean secondary or tertiary issues like "When was the Earth made? How about tattoos and alcohol? Do we have free will?" I mean essential core beliefs that define Christianity. Stuff like—Jesus was God and man, born of a virgin, died on a cross, resurrected, commands you to love your neighbor as yourself, instructs you to die to self, and asks that you create other followers.

The mark of today's Christian, however, is you do you. Be happy and believe whatever you want. Just be nice to each other and you'll reach the pearly gates. You may think I'm making this up, but in 2016, LifeWay Research confirmed the vast majority of self-identifying Christians believed this, and 73% of America claims they're Christians.

Most church services reinforce this focus on self. The vast majority of parishioners go to church to be entertained. If the music, sermon, or kids program isn't to their flavor, they bounce to a place that "feeds them." To keep numbers and donations coming, the church bends to the will of the congregation. So if the church reinforces a self-focus, then it's easy to judge and attack others because your needs matter most.[5]

Sledge says most Christians cannot even explain the gospel. Knowledge of the basic tenets of the Christian faith have not been properly taught from pulpits. Additionally, clear instructions from Scripture that all Christian denominations once agreed on have been reinterpreted consistent with the "Cult of Feel Good Deism." Today we have blatant violations of scriptural instructions "so no one is offended." Adherents to the reinterpretations are governed by their carnality, which causes great division in denominations and Christianity as a whole. Consider how grievously Jesus is offended by these scriptural deviations that actually put those He died to set free back into bondage.

We have come far away from the knowledge that the gospel is *meant to be offensive*. The gospel is meant to show sinful people their reality while offering a way of freedom from the consequences of sin, through faith in Christ.

It is a sad reality that church leadership has utterly offended the Christ whom they claim to serve, while seeking not to offend people with the expectation of attracting them to Christ.

In the next three chapters, we will explore various ways we can find remedies to our failures and follies, and restore the Church in both practice and image.

CHAPTER SIX

Attend the Wounded

Many people today are hostile towards Christianity and the people who profess the Christian faith, because of watered-down, offensive doctrine or the way Christians blatantly attack sinful people. In Chapter Three we identified the various groups where there is low esteem for Christianity and those people groups who claim no religious affiliation. We need to understand the people groups if we want to attract them for Christ.

The apostle Paul during his visit at Mars Hill is our model regarding the importance of knowing our audience—that is the person or people group we are trying to reach. Mars Hill is the Roman name for a hill in Athens, Greece. It is also called the Hill of Acres or the Areopagus. Mars Hill was the meeting place for the Areopagus Court, considered to be the highest court in Greece, hearing civil, criminal, and religious matters. Mars Hill was an important meeting place where philosophy, religion, and law were discussed.

As we learn from Acts chapter 17, Mars Hill is the location where the apostle Paul delivered one of his most important gospel presentations during his second missionary journey. The Greeks had altars to all their many gods and one to the "Unknown God." The apostle Paul begins his address by commending the people for being very religious, based on the many altars including one to the Unknown God. Paul then wisely used this altar as an appeal to the Greeks as he proclaimed to them the One True God and how they could be reconciled to Him. Paul's sermon is a classic example of how we need to present the gospel *beginning* with understanding of the beliefs of the person or people we are engaged with, and how to present the gospel in a logical and biblical fashion, with respect for the people. Paul's appeal is a classic example of apologetics in action. He reasoned with the people then presented the gospel, so the people could rationally determine which seemed the better "truth."

Appealing to unbelievers with an understanding of what they believe, being respectful in every way while engaging them and presenting the gospel from a position clearly communicated as caring and loving is the example we must follow if we want to attract people to Jesus.

Mindset of Those Who Leave the Church

Previous chapters have provided ample evidence of the increasing rejection of the Christian faith. The reasons for rejection are largely a failure by the Church. With this in mind, let us learn what we can to understand those we have wounded.

J. Warner Wallace wrote an opinion piece that was published on the Fox News internet site, about the failure in effectively teaching about God:

> The teaching they [people who leave the church] question seems to be about the *existence of God.* . . . When Christians walk away from the faith, more often than not, it's due to some form of *intellectual skepticism.* Ex-Christians often describe religious beliefs as innately blind or unreasonable.

When asked *why* they didn't believe, many said their views about God had "evolved" and some reported having a "crisis of faith." Their specific explanations included the following statements."

"Learning about evolution when I went away to college."

"Religion is the opiate of the people."

"Rational thought makes religion go out the window."

"Lack of any sort of scientific evidence of a creator."

"I just realized somewhere along the line that I didn't really believe it."

"I'm doing a lot more learning, studying and kind of making decisions myself rather than listening to someone else." [1]

Properly teaching the Word of God must be a priority for any pastor or teacher. At the same time, Christians are to be as the Bereans, searching Scriptures for ourselves to confirm if what we have been taught is accurate or not. Unfortunately, our society has become accustomed to deductive instruction instead of inductive.

Wounded By the Church

It is one thing to use statistics in our understanding of why people leave the Church, but hearing the heart and experiences of those who have left allows us direct compassionate insight as opposed to impersonal statistics.

In seeking to learn why people leave the church, I found two factions attempting to provide explanation. One was from the church management perspective and the other from the individual parishioner's perspective. Both provide insight and both should be considered if we genuinely want to reach people for Christ.

One blog I found collected testimonials from individuals opening their hearts and sharing their wounds imposed by the church they attended. Some experiences are not widespread realities of the majority of local churches. However, since all Christians comprise the Church, the wounds are suffered by all. The comments also show why the world of unbelievers feels justified in their rejection of the Church. What follows are paraphrased reasons individuals gave for leaving the church.

> The church I attended imposed pressure to be perfect and that created an atmosphere of judgmentalism. I'm not sure I'll ever be able to go back. I miss the familiarity, but certainly not the sickening atmosphere of lies.

> I left because my youth pastor betrayed me. I sought him out for counsel that he said would "be between us and God." A week or two later the whole congregation knew what I'd shared.

> It became obvious to me that the organized church was nothing more than a social club. We tithed to pay the costs to operate the club that had no widows, orphans, or hungry people to serve so we just kept serving ourselves.

> I left because the questions I asked were met with judgment as if I was rebelling. I simply had honest questions. Now I have to start all over again to find a place where I can feel safe and get my questions answered without being slapped on the side of the head with Bible verses. I wish the older generations could see that having questions does not equate to rebellion.

At my church it was never about relationship, but numbers. While I was "welcomed" at my church I wasn't received. Even after attending the church for five years, serving as a volunteer in different ways, people would still ask me at Sunday service if this was my first day. I also became sick and tired of the agenda-driven services where I heard more about abstaining from sex before marriage than about Jesus. I was so sick of the masks, the facades, and the show. All I wanted was to be part of a community of people where I could give what I have to offer and receive where I have need. The church broke my heart and I left. Even so, I realize the church is the only thing that will help bring healing to my brokenness.

I was born and raised in the church, baptized, confirmed, and married in the church. We had our kids baptized and confirmed in the church. I practically lived, breathed, ate, and slept church. Then our pastor sexually harassed me. My husband and I had to go through so much to get anything done about the harassment, even with hard evidence. We experienced the ugly, ugly underbelly at the highest leadership levels. We left that denomination for another and within six months the offending pastor resigned due to clergy sexual misconduct. The whole ordeal was a farce. The truth was silenced. Our family was slandered even though I had convincing evidence. Many people sided with the "poor" pastor who refused therapy. I don't know if I'll ever be able to trust a faith leader again.

These stories reveal the hypocrisy, the lack of integrity, and blatant sin in the Church. Scriptures are very clear that God holds leaders in the Church to a higher standard. James 3:1 reads, "Not many of you should become teachers my brothers, for you know that we who teach will be judged with greater strictness." When a church leader fails, the pain is felt by the entire congregation and their families, and potentially the entire community.

Church Blind Spots

In 2017 LifeWay Research conducted a survey to learn the reasons why young adults (ages twenty-three to thirty) leave the church. One of the more interesting findings was 70 percent cited political and spiritual concerns as reasons for their departure, significantly higher than the 52 percent who provided that same reason ten years prior.[2] The top five reasons given with this survey were as follows:

- I moved to college and stopped attending church (34 percent).
- Church members seemed judgmental or hypocritical (32 percent).
- I didn't feel connected to people in my church (29 percent).
- I disagreed with the church's stance on political/social issues (25 percent).
- My work responsibilities prevented me from attending (24 percent).

In an opinion article published on Fox News, "Five Reasons People Leave the Church," Andy Stanley wrote, "While many of us have been working hard to make church more interesting, it turns out that fewer people are actually interested." Stanley provided five reasons why people are leaving the church based on his research and interviews, which are summarized below.

1. We tell people that the Bible is the basis of Christianity.

The Bible is not the basis for Christianity, Jesus is. When our faith stands on anything other than Christ, we put ourselves (and others) in a position to fall. [Higher criticism of the Bible, points of scholarly disagreement, lack of scientific support of biblical claims can be cited as reasons to reject the Bible. Whereas the love of Christ is not something easily rejected.]

2. They believe suffering disproves the existence of God.

Our God promised there would be suffering until he makes all things new.

3. They had a bad church experience.

If our actions are rooted in Jesus' command to love one another (John 13:34), we can prevent many of the experiences that lead people away from his body.

4. We're bad at making people feel welcome.

It wasn't just his message that made Jesus irresistible. It was Jesus himself. People who were nothing like him, liked him. As followers of Jesus, we should be known as people who like people who are nothing like us.

5. We made *ekklesia* (the church) a building.

An *ekklesia* was a gathering of people for a specific purpose. Any specific purpose. It's not a building. It's not a physical location. It's a group of people. It's a lot easier to stop showing up at a place than it is to disconnect from a group of people who intimately know, love, and support each other.

If we want people to stop leaving the church—if we want Christianity to be irresistible again to the world—then maybe it's time to take another look at the movement Jesus started 2,000 years ago.[3]

Restorative Work of the Church

The Church, which includes all Christians, has a tremendous task before us to restore ourselves as leaders and restore individual Christians. We need to be soberly aware that each of us gives an account to God. How we relate one to another is a measure Jesus emphasized. Matthew 25:31–46 should be a hallmark guide for us all.

What is in our hearts, and what we understand to be true, whether it is true or not, determines our behavior. The following is the testimony of Pastor Josh Lotzenhiser, providing an example of how incorrect teaching, a desire to discover truth, and how compassionate mentoring restored a wounded soul producing a godly man who is on fire for Jesus.

> My parents were amazing in the way they raised my brothers and me in the church and creating a value for the things of God. Unfortunately, the teachings I received led me to perceive God as judgmental and angry with me, always left me feeling like I wasn't quite good enough for His acceptance. The love and grace of Jesus was foreign to me. I never really had a relationship with Jesus. I didn't read my bible, go to church and serve out of love for my Savior but rather out of duty and works. I believed in Jesus but it was really more because I didn't want to go to hell. I never really knew who He was or rather, who He is.
>
> However, July 4th, 2005 I had a radical experience with the love of God that changed my life. I stumbled into the Anaheim Convention Center during a "Believers Convention" as they were called and Brother Kenneth Copeland was preaching. I don't really remember what was said but I remember sitting in the back and having the feeling like Jesus was sitting in the same seat as me.

My heart burned, I felt His tangible love and my life has never been the same. This is the day I fully surrendered to Jesus, and I determined to serve Him the rest of my life.

After this encounter, I decided I would live my life for Him. I became a missionary, traveling to countries such as Thailand, Pakistan and Burma. These were some incredible times of seeing the power of God through miracles and salvations. I learned so much during this time, it was tremendous.

However, deep under the surface, I was still very much struggling. The years of instruction from church leadership emphasizing "works" was ingrained in me. While I was struggling to "get it right," I perceived all pastors and leaders of churches as an elite crop of Christians It didn't seem like they had any challenges—it seemed they were able to obey all of God's commands and live the Christian life with ease. I certainly couldn't.

In all my pursuit of God and His Kingdom, I still did not understand His grace. I didn't understand righteousness. I read the Bible hours a day, thinking that was what I had to do. I prayed for hours each day, thinking that was the right thing to do, I tithed, I gave all my money away, even gave my car away—really. It made me feel better for a moment but then I secretly despised this "Christian life." I didn't want any of my friends to experience what I was suffering. I did my best to do all the things my pastor said to do. I did my best to obey all of God's law. All I ended up with was condemnation, which led to secret sin, frustration, and discouragement. I wondered how these pastors were able to do it.

I concluded I wasn't going to be successful in ministry and I would always live with this struggle. Don't get me wrong, I saw hundreds of salvations (I worked to evangelize people on the street every Saturday, because I was told I had to). I saw many miracles. In fact, I saw a young girl who was born blind and without pupils in her eyes radically healed in a small village in Thailand. I saw the joy and excitement in her as she saw her mom for the first time. This was crazy and amazing. I was being used by God in powerful ways, but I had no peace inside. I had no rest. It was a constant work for me to keep God happy and pleased with me, or so I wrongly perceived.

Eleven years of struggle, I almost lost my marriage. I stopped going to church, stopped serving in ministry, and went back to the business world to make money. However, Jesus never stopped pursuing me. He never gave up on me. Then one day I found myself planting a church in downtown Chicago with some very dear friends and mentors. This brought me back to ministry and also back to this struggle.

I decided I had enough of this and sought Jesus for help. I poured out my heart to Him, I told Him all of my struggles (which was not something I ever did because I'd always been instructed "just have faith.") I read the book of Acts, and learned about the power and fruit of God in the men and women who believed Him. I saw their transformation and I wanted that. I saw that they were used by God but they were also full of peace and rest and enjoyed the Christian life. Sitting on my couch praying, I told God I would not leave until He spoke to me. I started to pray.

About thirty seconds later I heard God speak inside me in the loudest voice I had ever heard from Him—not an audible voice but an inward witness. All He said was, "I love you son." Boom! Life changed. At that moment, I had a revelation of God's love for me detached from my performance and works. He loved me period. He accepted me because of Jesus' perfect work.

In that moment the Holy Spirit revealed to me my entire past. In an instant He showed me everything I had done "for Him." He revealed all the works I had done to please Him and gain acceptance from Him was in vain. His work on the cross and grace to give me faith is all that is needed. Finally, I was able to cease from dead works and bask in Jesus' perfect work of the cross.

He showed me that in spite of every sin—He loved me. All the works and everything I was doing in the name of religion did nothing to add to His great love for me. In that moment, He removed the weight of the world off my shoulders. All the pressure of performance, all the demands I thought I had to fulfill, He wiped away. For the first time in my life I knew what it felt like to be free. I am loved by God, period. I was and am transformed by His love, just like the men and women in the book of Acts.

I asked Him, what next? He spoke to me again within my being, wanting me to reach out to an old acquaintance who I hadn't spoken to in years. We had gone to the same church years before. He was a business owner who advised me when I had my auto detailing business. I called him and said I felt led to call him. He just happened to have about 3 hours in his schedule free and came over to my house to talk. He brought in about 5 books authored by Joseph Prince and told me to read them. We sat for the next 3 hours talking about grace.

Learning about grace made me mad (actually it made my fleshly pride mad). It was tough. I seriously struggled with it. It went against everything I had learned doctrinally over the past 11 years! For the next 6 months I did nothing but study Romans and Galatians. I was renewing my mind and for the first time in my life I was truly beginning to fall in love with this Jesus—full of grace and truth. The transformation I experienced by the love and grace of God finally set me free from so manty of the struggles I had with sin. I no longer served out of duty, now I am motivated to serve out of love for Him.

Today, as associate pastor, I do my best to be transparent and authentic with my audience, no matter the size. I know what it's like to think that the preacher is somehow able to live the Christian life, but I can't. It has never been about our ability to do—it has always been about Christ in us and our trust in Him. It's not about performance, but relationship. We need more authenticity in the church today, no need to pretend that you are alright and without struggles. No need to put on a "strong face" in church because you are worried what others think of you. Just be real, there is healing in authenticity, there is power in being real and asking for help. Leaders, be you and preach Jesus.

Reaching Those Who Reject Christianity

First, I must point out the obvious to make certain we own our part. People in our culture who reject Christianity are rejecting Christ. This has happened on the Church's watch. The Church should respond with tremendous repentance and intercessory prayer. God is exceedingly long-suffering; as in many other times of human history, He responds without delay when we genuinely call out to Him for forgiveness and restoration.

All human beings are created with an innate desire to discover God. We each want to belong and be part of something that is greater than ourselves, and has lasting, worthwhile impact. We want our lives to have meaning and significance. Millennials and Generation Z often feel frustrated and dissatisfied without meaning and significance; this is good because we can address their felt needs.

I like to begin with a respectful acknowledgement of their frustration and with hope-filled questions because that immediately begins dialogue. I seek to show compassion and respect from the premise of God inviting us to reason with Him (Isa. 1:18). I ask questions such as:

- Why would you feel any sense of insignificance unless you were created to be significant?
- Do you have hope for finding something better or more to life?
- Who in this room wants to live your life on the basis of lies?

These type of questions allow honest dialogue to take place. The first question addresses the reality of a creator and how God created us with significance. The second question sparks hope even in one in despair, which reveals an innate hope to be more than our natural-born, sinful selves. The third question which no one ever says "Yes" to reveals how we universally prefer truth because we innately believe truth is good and lies are bad. This in turn reveals we all have an innate moral compass allowing us to know right from wrong.

These are simply touch points to begin conversation that can lead to a proper sharing of the gospel.

Reaching Millennials and Gen Z

Concerning millennials, we need to know they are all about integrity, transparency, honesty, grace, and truth. Millennials need to know we are genuine and authentic. Character matters greatly to this group, even more than competency. At the same time, they demand competency. As Carey Nieuwhof wrote: "This is, after all, a generation that has been marketed to more than any generation in human history. They can smell cheese and incompetence a mile way. But they can also smell fake a mile away. Being real matters more than doing. But doing still matters."[4]

Relationships are very important to millennials. This is great news allowing us to connect and mentor or disciple them. Millennials prefer to emphasize Jesus over God, because Jesus is more relatable having lived the human existence. This group also wants to be part of a passionate cause that makes a difference for the better, and they are not adverse to taking risks. They want to jump in and be part of the mission as the focus, believing money will follow. I find this an interesting because this is a demonstration of faith that many money-focused churches do not have. [5]

Regarding Generation Z, Octavio Esqueda believes our "post-Christian" culture provides a great opportunity for followers of Christ to shine amidst a society that desperately needs Jesus. While the gospel is no longer accepted as the mainstream message, Christians can follow the example of the early church by demonstrating their love for one another. Modeling Christ to everybody is important, but especially to Gen Zers.

Churches can help Gen Zers by displaying a worldview that promotes Christian virtues that speak to their compassion and concern for others. Additionally, this generation is uniquely poised to help older generations embrace those who are different from them. Adults can teach Gen Zers how genuine Christian love is rooted in truth.

One area that will stretch the Church is Gen Zer's acceptance of sexual and gender confusion. Gen Zers seems to have a tendency towards evolving views about sexuality, out of a great desire to empathize with marginalized groups. Empathy is a valued character trait among Gen Zers.

Referring to the Barna Research, Esqueda wrote:

> Nowdays there is a need for radical discipleship where followers
> of Christ live their lives surrendered to the Holy Spirit in complete
> obedience to their Lord. In many instances young people do not
> reject Christ, but do reject a sociological and political
> interpretation of Christianity that they see in their parents or
> adults around them and that do not necessarily reflect biblical
> values. A post-Christian context forces believers to be completely
> committed followers of Christ.[6]

It seems the apathy and complacency of the older generations has created
a vacuum where genuine, authentic Christian faith is desperately needed. This
means the first step to helping others find Christ is to get our faith life in
order. Perhaps this is how God is causing the older and younger generations
to work together according to Acts 2:17–18:

> And in the last days it shall be, God declares, that I will pour out
> my Spirit on all flesh, and your sons and your daughters shall
> prophesy, and your young men shall see visions, and your old men
> shall dream dreams; even on my male servants and female
> servants in those days I will pour out my Spirit, and they shall
> prophesy.

In the next chapter, we will consider what the Church can do to prevent
some of the painful issues discussed in this chapter.

CHAPTER SEVEN

Identify Remedies

We've explored why Christians are leaving the Church, and why people refuse to consider the Church. So now let us give them reasons to seriously reconsider. To accomplish this there needs to be both a personal and a corporate effort. Individual Christians must confidently know why they are committed to the Christian faith. Church leadership needs to make certain their congregation is *objectively* confident of their faith. If we are going to provide answers the world of unbelievers needs, we must provide objective evidence which can be verified. Subjective reasons for faith cannot be verified.

While I wholly embrace the charismatic experience, I also believe we must balance the subjective experience with objective evidence to best practice what the Christian faith offers and be able to share our faith with unbelievers.

Science, Reason, and Faith

In the previous chapter, J. Warner Wallace helped us understand the two main reasons why people leave the church:

- Lack of evidence for the existence of God
- Intellectual skepticism

Most people today do not understand the rich, evidential history of Christianity. Wallace published an excellent article addressing the popular thought that science and reason are completely incompatible with Christian belief. He has provided a summary list of great Christian thinkers and scientists.[1] He wrote:

> The psalmist appealed to the design and fine-tuning of the universe to demonstrate the existence of God (Psalm 19:1). Jesus appealed to both eyewitness testimony (John 16:8) and the indirect evidence of his miracles (John 10:38) to argue for the authority of his statements. The disciples identified themselves as eyewitnesses and appealed to their observations of the Resurrection to make the case for the Deity of Jesus (Acts 4:33).
>
> Ex-Christians often leave the Church because they don't think anyone in the Church can answer their questions or make a case. It's time for believers to accept their responsibility to explain what Christianity proposes and why these propositions are true, especially when interacting with young people who have legitimate questions. Rather than embracing a blind or unreasonable faith, Christians must develop an informed, forensic faith that can stand up in the marketplace of ideas.[2]

I agree entirely with Wallace; the responsibility is on us—all who are genuine Christians—to be ready to provide good reason for our faith as 2 Timothy 4: 2–5 implores us:

Preach the word; be ready in season and out of season; reprove, rebuke, exhort, with great patience and instruction. For the time will come when they will not endure sound doctrine; but wanting to have their ears tickled, they will accumulate for themselves teachers in accordance to their own desires, and will turn away their ears from the truth and will turn aside to myths. But you, be sober in all things, endure hardship, do the work of an evangelist, fulfill your ministry.

Ask most Christians why they are Christians and they cite a variety of reasons:

- Because of the Bible.
- Because a valued and trusted person in my life taught me to believe.
- I was born into a Christian home, so I am Christian.

If you tell a person who does not believe that the Bible is the unique, authoritative document and the basis of your faith, they will consider you utterly daft. Believing in Christianity on the basis of what a trusted person such as a parent or pastor has taught us is only a starting point. What is more important is to examine what we are taught to make certain it is accurate. Believing you are a Christian because of your parent's faith is unfounded for each of us must make a commitment of faith on our own.

Know What You Believe and Why

My first book in this Faith to Live By series, is an apologetic treatment of the basic questions unbelievers have. I start with the examination of truth and relativism, then explore religious pluralism, and provide a chapter for each of the five major world religions and one on New Age philosophy so people can see the stark differences in the various religions and the character of the religion's god. Then, using extra-biblical, historical evidence I satisfy questions about the supremacy of the Bible in contrast to all other documents of religious authority; Jesus' claims to be God; and the resurrection.

While I wrote the book for skeptics, reviews indicated committed Christians have gained depth to their understanding of Christianity, allowing them to boldly share their faith. In addition to ensuring individual Christians are knowledgeable and confident about the reasons for their faith, church leaders need to assess their own collective leadership.

Individual Church Culture Audit

The Church needs to conduct a cultural audit. In the same way Pastor Farrar and his board of elders had to examine themselves regarding ministering to Walt/Laura, church leadership needs to evaluate their practices and policies. Questions to ask might include:

- What evidences do we have that our congregation is properly knowledgeable about the Christian faith?
- What are we doing to ensure each member of the church is discipled?
- Are we truly a welcoming church, wanting all to join us, or do we prefer the comfort and familiarity of our congregation as it is?
- Are we properly receptive of people who have questions? Have we made a safe environment for people to inquire?
- Are we willing to receive people through our doors who are clearly different from us?
- Do we have a culture of exclusivity or piety as believers?

- Is our congregation a community as a whole or do we have cliques and factions?

- Are we staying true to Scripture or have we adopted our own doctrine?

- What real-world life issues are we ill equipped to provide ministry and help for?

- Do we have sufficient accountability practices in place for both leadership and church members?

- Do we teach relationship Christianity or performance Christianity?

- Are we an outreach church visible to the community or are we an in-reach church with little influence on our community?

- Do we have a method of intentionally integrating visitors to help them know about our church culture in order to decide to join?

- Are we actively engaged in the mandate from Matthew 28:18–20?

- Do we express the unconditional love of Jesus, or do we expect certain standards or beliefs to be in place to include people?

Evaluating your church culture should also include a willingness to poll your congregation. It is difficult to be objective when you are the object. I was part of a steering committee at my home church. There were two things we did to get an outsider's view of our church culture:

1. We had a member of our denominational headquarters secretly visit our church to provide an extensive evaluation.
2. We created a survey and asked our congregation members to anonymously complete the questionnaire.

Yes, the above steps take courage. However, the choice is to be courageous and learn our shortcomings, or keep our head in the sand and do church as usual. Given the many evidences of the failure of the Church attracting people, I suggest a church culture audit be done annually. If you would like a copy of the two questionnaires we used, feel free to contact me.

Adopt the Early Church Devotion

I personally believe the present time is urgent. The Church must prepare for the end-time harvest by first becoming all Jesus intended the Church to be, so that the Church is viewed as the relevant source for discovering truth, hope, and freedom in Christ. This can be accomplished through humbling ourselves before the Lord, or waiting on His judgment. I am hoping, praying, and offering this book so it can be the first option.

Using the early church as our model, we can identify much of what we must do to revitalize the Christian faith. I especially liked what Bock and Cooke shared. In wanting to find a time when the Church was vital and relevant, they looked back through history. They found it necessary to go back to the early church, over 2,000 years ago.

Let us have a proper understanding of the people who were part of the early church. They had no money, no political power, no plans, and no education, no internet and no cell phones. Yet within 200 years they went from nothing to the most influential force in the western hemisphere. What made it possible for them to become so influential? Bock said in an interview, "They were all-in. They were 100 percent committed, even if it meant their death, and many times it did. Yet, they were fully committed."[3] They laid down their own will and ideals, preferring instead the will and ideals of Jesus.

The theme of being "all-in" is one I repeatedly encountered in recent weeks. When I write books or messages, I prayerfully partner with the Lord and listen to know what's on His heart that He wants me to address. The title of a recent message I prepared was "With God it Is All or Nothing." In preparing to write the message, I came across a prophetic word from Lana Vawser. She wrote:

> The fear of the Lord came upon me strongly as I heard Him speak "The Church is not ready yet, sound the alarm to 'make yourself ready' through your yielding to Me, My Spirit and My way. I will make My people ready!"
>
> People of God, it's time that we cry out to the Holy Spirit and invite Him to reveal to us whatever needs to be done or dealt with to make us ready for what He is going to do in this new era. It is not about 'getting everything right' it's about a heart position, it's about obedience and surrender to His way, His process and His Spirit. The key is inviting the Holy Spirit to do whatever He needs to do to make us ready and not ignore His voice, His conviction or His process. The fear of the Lord came upon me strongly as I heard Him speak, "The Church is not ready yet, sound the alarm to 'make yourself ready' through your yielding to Me, My Spirit and My way. I will make My people ready![4]

Questions I encouraged attendees to ask themselves to evaluate their level of surrender were:

- What has occupied my thoughts, or entered my heart that has prevented me from being prepared?
- What have I accepted as truth that is actually a contradiction to God's Word?
- What is keeping me from being wholehearted with God?

Proverbs 29:18 says: "Where there is no prophetic vision the people cast off restraint, but blessed is he who keeps the law." Similarly Hosea 4:6 reads: "My people are destroyed for lack of knowledge; because you have rejected knowledge, I reject you from being a priest to me. And since you have forgotten the law of your God, I also will forget your children."

The greatest commandment of the New Testament Law is "You shall love the Lord your God with all your heart and with all your soul and with all your mind. This is the great and first commandment" (Matt. 22:37–38)

And let us make special note, God addresses *His people*, not unbelievers, in both the above Proverbs and Hosea passages.

Astounding Faith

The early church Christians were known by their love, Bock explained in an interview. He cited the same issue of Roman infanticide noted by Sledge in Chapter Five. The love for the abandoned Roman babies, and other loving deeds the early Christians showed, attracted the world to know more about the motivation behind their love.

What can the Church do today to astound the world? Bock and Cooke's previously mentioned book offers about ten ideas as starting points to energize Christians to come up with more ideas. During Bock's interview he cited the American foster care system as one example. He explained there are currently about 450,000 children in the foster care system now. That is about the same as the population of Salt Lake City. The extremely sad statistics of the foster care system reveals 15 percent of these kids will be homeless within one year of entering the system. About 75 percent of girls in the system will be pregnant by age 21. And only 1 percent of all these kids will graduate high school.

Bock explained there are about 350,000 churches in America and said, "If every church in America adopted one plus kid each, we could wipe out the system in just one year."[5] Think of how this demonstration of Christ's love would be received by the unchurched! Imagine how the millennials who are passionate about social justice would be astonished and likely attracted to explore the Christian faith afresh.[6]

Bock told how one year, just a couple days before Christmas, he placed a free ad on Craig's List asking for those parents who could not afford to supply their children with Christmas presents to contact him. The first year, he met a couple at Target and shopped the store for toys. When the toys were selected he then put groceries for a Christmas meal in the cart. Bock said he spent $300 that year. The astonished family asked him why he did it, which opened the door for him to share that Jesus was his motivation.

Bock has continued to do this each year, and has gained support from other friends who are doing the same. After ten years, they have collectively helped over 200 families, many who say once they get on their feet they plan to do the same thing. Not only are the family members astonished and then drawn to what motivates people to help strangers, but Target employees are too. Finding ways to demonstrate our faith that astonishes the world of unbelievers is an excellent way to begin demonstrating what the Christian faith is truly all about.

Let me tell you why Bock's generosity struck my heart chords. My husband David was hired by the managing partner involved with developing a large multi-planned, mixed community with a golf course. It was the dream job of a lifetime. We rented our home out, packed up our two toddler children and moved to the new community where we had no friends or family. Within the first year of David working on the project, he discovered serious wrongdoing by the financial partner. In short order, the project was seized by the federal government on seven counts of fraud. David, who was working for the managing partner, was not implicated, but still he and all others were immediately unemployed.

We had bought a new home in this new community and had no financial staying power. We were forced to sell everything we could live without, ultimately losing our new home to foreclosure. This was during the early 1990s when the job and financial markets took a serious hit. Our ordeal lasted four very long years and took a serious toll on every aspect of our family.

Christmas after Christmas came around with our having no ability to provide toys for our children or celebrate the holiday as we'd like. As parents in our affluent American culture with its holiday traditions, this was exceedingly debilitating. We who had once enjoyed a six-figure income were living off of menial part-time jobs and the generosity of people who would bring us groceries or provide us checks or money orders. One Christmas a woman I knew asked me if she could hide her kids' Christmas presents in our garage. Imagine what it was like for me and my children to enter the garage and get in my car to take them to school, walking past multiple huge Toys R Us bags.

In that season God taught us a great deal. One important life lesson is each of us must live our life without comparing ourselves to others. Another is love and trust in God are decisions we make by faith. What I knew about God, and seeking His help to persevere, allowed us to remain faithful through it all, and in the end experience His reward according to Hebrews 11:6.

The people who observed and even helped is in this long season, have remarked that our steadfast demonstration of faith has encouraged them in their own times of trial.

In the past, hospitals and universities were established by Christians. These institutions were tremendously needed by society and were therefore embraced. These two examples serve as reminders of how much impact for the good of society and culture Christianity can have. Unfortunately Christian apathy through the years means these institutions founded by Christians have been taken over by secular ideal and other ideals actually hostile to the Christian faith. It is imperative the Church become engaged in society and culture in astounding ways if we want to partner with Jesus in the end-times' harvest of souls.

Astounding acts of service need not be public. A simply act of kindness done in secret often has a ripple effect. The people Bock had helped at Christmas let him know they wanted to do the same for others when they got back on their financial feet. If our motive for serving others is to get personal recognition, our motive is wrong. As Christians we are to serve the Lord through serving others so they see our good deeds and glorify God (Matt. 5:16). The idea is simply to provide a good deed or service that would cause a non-believer to wonder *What is their motivation?* The selfless kindness will not only bless them but attract them to want to know more.

Personal Not Vicarious Involvement

The early church did not have any of the modern communication advantages we have. Yet in approximately 200 years the early believers supported a movement that became the greatest influence on the western hemisphere. How did they do it? By each individual being engaged in demonstrating their faith.

Today we have largely stepped back from personal involvement with those who are marginalized or disadvantaged. The Church as a whole mostly offers assistance to those in our culture in need through major institutions. The Salvation Army, Childcare Worldwide, Food for the Hungry, and Samaritan's Purse are excellent examples of Christian organizations many Christians support and look to in providing for others. While this is good, and we should continue supporting these organizations, unbelievers do not necessarily credit the good these organizations do to Christianity. What is needed instead is for individuals to simply do what they can on a personal level. We need to be willing to "get our hands dirty."

Wasn't Jesus' life example one of personally getting involved with people? What can you do as an individual? One thing the Lord has inspired me with is a grass-roots campaign that I want to grow into producing regional events specifically to attract unbelievers. I am tired of the Church preaching to the choir and I want to help generate outreach events that meet the needs of people in the community.

I plan on providing kits local churches and Christian organizations can use to conduct their own events under my campaign brand "Come Back to God™." The focus is to reveal we are all made by God in His image to have relationship with Him. This is where all our genuine needs will be met. Each one needs to learn truth for himself or herself. By experiencing the love of Christ expressed by Christians, many will hopefully choose to come back to God.

Once there is sufficient local community momentum, then I'll ask these local "chapters" to assist me in conducting three regional events across America. We are planning this endeavor under Exceptional Keynote Speakers (EKS), a division of Pamela Christian Ministries, LLC.

On the surface it may sound like I have at least a medium-size organization. I do not. It is just me and my business partner, Keri Spring. But when a vision is from the Lord and properly cast, others will catch the vision and join in. The vision for "Come Back to God ™" is far bigger than I can personally accomplish, or fully know how to do. But any aspiration that is small enough for me to fulfill by my own means is not of God. It takes faith to step out into God's plan. If our faith in Him is properly established, then we know He will equip us for every good work to which He calls us. Fear and doubt are antithetical to faith.

You will be put to the test before you are to begin the work, as every prominent figure in the Bible was to whom God revealed His calling. God wants to make certain your faith is strong enough for the task. Faith is tested by opposition. I later realized this explained our four long years of under-employment and unemployment and the loss of so very much.

God may call you to start something or to support an effort already underway. If you want to know more about the outreach events via Exceptional Keynote Speakers, please email me at our general inbox info@ExceptionalKeynoteSpeakers.com or contact us through the web site at https://ExceptionalKeynoteSpeakers.com

There are many things you can do as an individual to reach the lost for Christ. Another ministry I have is called "Bag Ladies." It is not my original idea, but it is a great one. The entire church is invited to bring new travel-size toiletries, socks, washcloths, combs/brushes, razors, deodorant, toothbrushes, and more as well as individually-wrapped snacks. They drop them off at our church reception booth. Then every other month a team of ladies and myself organize and begin stuffing large zip bags with the items and a printed list of local soup kitchens and shelters. These packed bags are then made available at the reception booth for church members to pick up and keep in their car to bless a homeless person.

Serving the community's children is another area of involvement for our local churches. Vacation Bible schools are an excellent way to show the community your concern. As often both parents work, having a safe and fun place for their children to go for an entire week ministers to the whole family.

If you are not the visionary or entrepreneurial type, then helping with another person's vision may be perfect for you. All visionaries need as much practical support as possible.

Brainstorm the Possibilities

I encourage individuals to begin in their own neighborhoods, perhaps by asking their neighbors what their needs are. Do you even know your neighbors? Bock said he realized he did not know his neighbors so he and his wife organized a block party. It turned out most of the neighbors on the block did not know one another. After they became acquainted and were aware of one another's needs, they could become the arms and feet of Jesus to them. Meeting the needs of others includes: practical, emotional, mental, and spiritual needs. Beyond obvious basic needs such as food and clothing, people need companionship, to be valued, to be entertained, and so much more.

Consider the following ideas:

- Arrange a team of qualified people to paint the home of a single parent or elderly person.
- Organize a diaper or backpack drive and give what is collected to a suitable organization to distribute.
- Get inexpensive matching T-shirts made and go through your community together picking up trash.
- Show support for local pregnancy centers or women's shelters by doing a walk for their organization to raise awareness and potentially funds. Walk on major streets with matching T-shirts to raise awareness and secure donations.
- Arrange a scavenger hunt for the kids in an underprivileged neighborhood at a local park.
- Organize a team of men who are familiar with auto mechanics to help repair cars for widows and single women.

- Coordinate with your church children's department to help with age-appropriate support for your specific ministry service, teaching children from an early age the importance of being hands and feet for Jesus.
- Hold a picnic or BBQ open to the public on the church property or a nearby park.
- Hold a car show and BBQ.
- Hold a talent show inviting the locals with a prize for the winner.
- Offer a weekly walk for the benefit of exercise, letting the attendees know you are willing to pray for them.
- Host a softball game at a neighborhood park complete with snacks and maybe hotdogs.
- Organize a dog-walking service.
- Help end biblical illiteracy and hold a Bible study in your neighborhood.

There is a creative idea for every need.

Be wise about the legalities and find out if permits are required for what you have planned. Make sure liability insurance is in place if needed. Get recipients to sign a no-liability waiver for services provided, if warranted. Or partner with an existing paint contractor or auto mechanic, for example, so protections are in place. Be wise, keep the faith, and reject the fear.

If the ministry service is done under the banner of your local church, chances are you will have all the protections in place. Take your ideas to your pastor or church leader and decide what you can do to make the Church relevant today.

Church United—A Model for Today

I recently learned of a church that can serve as an excellent model for ideas and specific strategies for what you may consider doing in your church. Calvary Chapel in Fort Lauderdale, Florida is one of 150 area churches participating in the program that have put aside egos and logos for Jesus. Under the theme of "Connect, Collaborate, and Celebrate," Church United is working to make south Florida a better place to live. The churches have joined to promote the initiatives determined by the collective church leadership to address spiritual losses, social pain, and cultural brokenness.

Church United has a five-year strategic plan that began in 2017 with area pastors meeting to pray for the cities and communities of south Florida. These pastors, aware of the many social and cultural problems in their communities, gathered together to pray and identify where the Church is needed.

Working with LifeWay Research and Barna Research Group, they learned 76 to 78 percent of south Floridians self-identify as Christians. However, with further probing the learned only 3 percent are believing Christians who are influencing others for Christ.

By 2018, through prayer and much effort, Church United was formed with the focus of doubling the number of committed Christians over the next five years. They intentionally cast a vision so big that only God could fulfill it, and determined to trust God for the vision. These area churches are unified in evangelism, planting churches, developing leaders, mobilizing commerce, engaging with education, and equipping individuals to join in the effort to one day make south Florida the best place to live, work, and raise families. They are committed to making every individual Christian a leader in the community.

Each church uses its unique attributes and calling to fulfill the initiatives. When I spoke with Denise Trio, strategic development project manager for Calvary Chapel Fort Lauderdale, a Church United participant, I was wonderfully encouraged. I learned how the church, armed with knowledge of the conditions in their region, identified the areas and people groups they would reach for Christ. They established team leaders and formed teams under the banner of Vision 2023—a five-year plan to reach their goals.

They identified eight areas, referred to as buckets, where they want to make a difference. Under the spiritual bucket they have Church Planting and Next Gen teams. Under the social bucket they have a Recovery Team, Elder Care, and Marriage and Family. Under the cultural bucket they have a Business Engagement team and an Education team.

Church planting includes identifying and nurturing new leaders. Next Gen is an effort to reach children during their formative years with the gospel and making genuine disciples who will be less likely to abandon their faith when they are college age.

South Florida has a high percentage of substance abuse and rehabilitation centers. Calvary recognized this as an opportunity to work with the centers by bringing Bible studies to them. The church also has treatment programs for men and women on one of their campuses, such as Celebrate Recovery, that goes beyond recovery to making disciples. Elder Care was seen as an opportunity to take church to the residents in different facilities, which has resulted not only in ministering to the residents but to the staff and visiting families as well. Foster Care has led them to partner with other faith-based organizations such as 4-Kids of South Florida. The Marriage and Family team focus on rewriting the marriage narrative to create strong families, reduce divorce by emphasizing the importance of Jesus being the center of the family.

The Business Engagement team is needed because of the high rate of start-up business in the area that typically last only a few years before they close. Teams work with business leaders to help them use biblical principles in the management of money and the ethics of business. They hold regular events with speakers who are proven local business owners, raise up marketplace chaplains, and equip those who work in secular business to form Bible studies on lunch breaks, and in general infuse Scripture into the marketplace.

The Education team was needed because of the deplorable reality of public education in the area. Not only do the schools have poor grades for the students they turn out, the student/teacher ratio is untenable. The church doesn't believe Jesus should be banned from the classroom, so working with Christian teachers they develop creative ways to influence the kids for Christ, and offer weekly prayer meetings for the teachers. The team also provides support by rallying school social workers and working with them to provide Christ-centered counseling for emotional and social behavior. They've developed a curriculum titled "Real Essentials" that addresses social and emotional wellness courses based on Scripture. They also partner with other Christian organizations such as First Priority School Clubs for Christ, providing after-school Bible study programs and Fire Wall Centers, which is a mentoring/tutoring homework help for kids.

Going outside the four walls of the Church and infusing Christ in every area of life is precisely what we need to do in keeping with the Great Commission of Matthew 28:18–20.

Feed Your Personal Interests

You can see from this chapter, there are endless number of ideas you can come up with to be of help to others in the name of Jesus. Whatever you are good at, gifted with, and enjoy doing, consider how you can turn that into a ministry outreach.

God has given each of us a unique combination of spiritual gifts and natural talents, and He has a created purpose for our lives, established before we were conceived. When we are operating according to our gifts, talents, and purpose, life is the most fulfilling it can possibly be. Even if the task becomes laborious and requires sacrifice from us, when we are doing what we were created to do, there is no stopping us.

When I speak to various groups I often say, "Unless we are living according to God's intended purpose, using the spiritual gifts and natural talents He has given us, there is no real hope for finding genuine personal fulfillment." The younger generations who have been indoctrinated to believe we came from nothing and we will end in nothing have a difficult time bridging that belief with the innate desire to be significant—to experience self-actualization as discussed in chapter four. The reason they—and we all— seek to be significant *is because we are created by God to be significant*. The Christian faith fulfills every innate human need, and we have the chance to show those who don't know Christ this truth.

Each of us desires to discover our God-intended purpose and to live "in our element." Just as a fish out of water will not survive, neither will we thrive when we are operating outside of God's intended purpose for our lives. We are to live a life following Jesus' example. Like the early disciples, we need to be fishers of men. We do this by first addressing their practical needs. After winning their trust concerning our motives, we can establish a relationship that allows us to share Who motivates us to serve others.

Being Fully Surrendered

We most assuredly cannot say the Church in America is fully surrendered to Jesus. Yes, there are pockets, or various local churches that could easily be characterized as wholly committed, but we cannot say that characterizes the Church at large. The first focus needs to be on becoming fully surrendered to Jesus. How can we accomplish this? How do we take the Church from being largely indifferent, apathetic, and self-serving to being all-in? We need to be convicted.

The Holy Spirit is working on convicting us now, evidenced by the numbers of books and messages on the topic of reviving the Christian faith and Church. I believe the Holy Spirit is urging us to "get in the gym," as Bock would say, and do the hard work. Those who are prepared in advance of a crisis have the best ability to overcome.

Prepare the New Way of the Lord

God is calling out His people to lead the way of repentance and preparation. We will see increasing numbers of people appear on the scene, as modern-day John the Baptists, to proclaim the importance of being prepared. In this new era we are being charged with identifying what worked in prior times, to abandon what is not working in the present time, and prayerfully receive God's strategy to move forward. A shift is required from outdated ineffective traditions that hinder the cause of Christ to effective new methods. Often a new move of God is met with suspicion by church leadership and members. We humans are not fond of change, even if it is change for the better. We need to seek God in prayer for confirmation that this new way is indeed God bringing His desired change. Leaders who continue to resist the change may be those the Lord is calling out of leadership.

Much has been testified about "house churches" where the Holy Spirit is powerfully present. Church leaders who feel threatened by house churches, should take their concerns to the Lord. House churches could very well be one way the Lord reverses the decline of Christian adherents, since the traditional church is viewed as irrelevant. Rather than resist this potential movement, consider the wild success of the early church who met in house churches. The goal of church leadership must be to make disciples for Christ, not a congregation for themselves.

Andrew Whalen, a prophetic revivalist, said:

> On a recent "prayer drive," I heard the Holy Spirit say in my heart, "Wilderness." I thought to myself, *Oh no, God, not more wilderness.* And thankfully I heard more. He said, "I am about to visit the wilderness."
>
> A few days after the Lord told me that He was going to visit the wilderness, I was given a dream. In my dream, I saw that house churches and other less "organizational" places were being invaded by the Spirit of God. I saw what I knew to be thousands of people at a time packing into one house. I recognized that the focus of these house meetings was prayer.
>
> In one house, I saw that thousands were waiting in line to sit in a chair and receive prayer. After each person was prayed for they would get up and say, "I have never before been touched by God like that."
>
> After I woke from the dream, I was led to consider the visitation of God in the wilderness by John the Baptist. In Mark 1:5, "The whole Judean countryside and all the people of Jerusalem went out to Him. Confessing their sins, they were baptized by Him in the Jordan River."

I believe the dream of the "house churches" was both literal and symbolic. First, I believe that God is literally going to pour out His Spirit on prayer-focused house churches, and many will "go out" to find and encounter God in these lesser known places. Second, I believe the house churches may be symbolic for the less-conventional type places where the Church gathers. As God visits the "wilderness" I believe we are going to see barn revivals, house churches, Bible studies and prayer groups become the target of God's Spirit, and thousands will be drawn to find God in these places. Certainly we live in great days of transition and visitation.[7]

Andrew and his wife Kelly run Whalen Ministries which has pioneered a house of prayer, multiple campus ministries, a house church, revival networks, evangelism, prophetic roundtables, street evangelism and human trafficking intervention initiatives. Andrew travels nationally and internationally on prophetic assignments to pray, prophesy, and preach. He works in league with national prayer leaders, financial leaders, and even law enforcement to bring prophetic wisdom and breakthrough. The example of Whalen Ministries in this anti-Christian culture seems fitting for us to explore. Through prayer, and being open to the heart of God and His strategies for these wicked days, we can implement creative ways to impact our culture for Christ.

The next two chapters will provide ideas for help and recourses we can use as together we accomplish more.

CHAPTER EIGHT

Identify Resources and Partnerships

If Bock and Cooke's evaluation of the Church's time of greatest influence was that of the early church, let us examine what we can learn. As we read in Acts chapters 1 and 2 Christians were:

- Predominantly commoners without impressive credentials
- United in their faith as demonstrated by acts of service
- Known by their love
- Without a structure of hierarchy such as the Jews had
- Funded by pooling resources, caring for their own
- Led by apostle Peter, Christ's other disciples, and those appointed to leadership by the disciples
- Gathered together for worship and instruction in church homes
- Bold in their faith, even to the point of death.

For the most part, men and women of the early church did not seek positions of prominence. They did not seek the approval of men. Their whole devotion was to Jesus with an understanding of the profound redemption from sin and death that Jesus' life, death, and resurrection provided. They had understanding of the new life they had received with a confident faith that allowed them not to deny their faith, even in the face of death. I think the question for today is: *How can we impart that same depth of understanding about Jesus and all He offers in people's lives today?*

Create a Community Centered on Jesus

The most immediate resource for any church is to partner with their congregation members. Establishing standards of conduct and accountability should be predominate and values regularly discussed. Creating a healthy community centered on Jesus needs to be an ongoing effort, fortified with regular assessments to avoid becoming complacent and falling into error.

Watching the deterioration of our culture and society, for the past five years I have been praying for the Lord to expose corruption and replace it with righteous men and women. We certainly have seen a lot exposed. Because of media's bias, I do not believe we have been informed of just how much and from what camps. We know of some of the Lord's housecleaning in the removal of some Christians from leadership that did make media coverage. How much better it would be if church leaders established mutual accountability, with checks and balances, quietly applying church discipline when and where needed, for the safety of the entire congregation. This must be motivated by love at all times to prevent falling into legalism.

Carey Nieuwhof helped us understand some of the reasons church leaders fall in Chapter Five. However, I think if all churches would make Jesus the center of their community instead of the pastor, the worship team, the teacher, or any other individuals, we would experience significant change in the right direction. Consider what I mentioned before about having a "secret shopper" from your denomination, or another individual who can provide you with an honest assessment of your church. Again, it is hard to be objective when you are the object.

Some churches I have attended are very warm and welcoming from the parking lot into the sanctuary. Others have cliques and a sense of various divisions or camps within. I believe what makes the Bible study organization the success it is stems from their enforced guidelines to remain focused on the reason we gather—to grow in our knowledge and relationship with Jesus and one another, regardless of our respective denominations. When we focus on our reason for coming together and what we have in common, we create a community of unity, and that is exactly what Jesus wants.

Church leadership needs to better educate their congregants to own their Christian influence upon the world. Ministry and evangelism is not the job of church leadership—it is the role of all Christians. Christians should not come to church to be entertained, but to be equipped and enlightened to better influence the world where they live. Congregation members should have a clear understanding of their role as individual Christians and as members of their church community.

The "flavor" of the community of each church will be different because of the dynamics within the particular group. Based on the listing of seven church cities in the book of Revelation, it seems different flavors are to be expected. However, let us remain aware of the condition of our local church, and remain true to Jesus, our first love above all else.

Division of Labor

I have been in more than one church that neglected the contributions I could make for the operations of the church. I am educated, qualified, and experienced to do a number of things. Whether it is intentional neglect or unintentional oversight, I know I am not the only one who is underutilized.

This is a serious concern for me and it ought to be for the Church at large.

- What are the reasons current church leadership does not more fully engage the members of the congregation?
- Why are increasing numbers of Christian pastors and leaders burning out and leaving their leadership positions?
- Are leaders so controlling they are unwilling to engage the help of others?
- Are leaders finding their identity in their leadership positions instead of in Christ?

These and other similar questions should be part of the previously recommended church audit.

By following the example of the early church we should assess the giftings and abilities of those in our congregations and allow them a place of service in the body of Christ. The local church should identify what areas of service and support are needed, then offer training for church members qualified to step into these positions. The absolute best resources for the church are its members.

Training and Equipping

I am baffled by the constant "reinventing of the wheel" that goes on in the church. It is as if every church works to have its own brand, even within the same denomination. I am also amazed at the lack of acceptance of parachurch organizations I have seen. From personal experience I can say this leaves the local church ill-equipped to meet many of the real-world needs people sitting in the pews have.

My husband and I needed genuine counseling to help us in our marriage a number of years ago. We went to our church to get help from the pastor assigned to help married couples. This church would be considered a mega-church where church leadership cannot personally know all the members. After a very brief conversation with the pastor, our first meeting ended with us being handed workbooks to individually complete. The booklets contained a myriad of personal questions. At the next meeting, the first words from the pastor were, "I have never seen two married people who are further apart in their responses as you." So much for an encouraging word.

We then went to our former pastor, who knew us quite well. He listened. However, he had to admit he had absolutely no training or education in order to help us, neither did he have anyone on staff who could help. The issues in our marriage were not obscure or unique in any way. They were very common problems the majority of married couples experience. Clearly, the two churches did not have the answers we needed when they should have. Why would we as Christians go to a secular marriage counselor to get the help needed? Why doesn't the local church make it a priority to understand the majority of real-life issues where counseling help will be needed and establish proper staff, or at least have recommended referrals? Notwithstanding liability exposure, there may be several areas of pastoral care, mentoring, and discipleship where congregational members are qualified and can provide the services as volunteers.

Again, considering the great last-days harvest, now is the time for the Church to get prepared. Consider the following list of real-life needs and identify if you have staff or a ministry you can recommend should a member of your church seek help with the need. This is not an exhaustive list. And while we would like to think these and others issues are not issues among Christians, they are.

- **Addictions:** alcoholism, cocaine, drug, food, gambling, gaming, heroin, internet, marijuana, meth, nicotine, opioid, prescription drug, sex, shopping, work.
- **Sexual Issues:** gender identity, transgender, homosexuality, pedophilia.
- **Marriage Relations:** celibacy, pre-marital, adultery, financial, marriage counseling, intimacy, trust.
- **Family Relations:** domestic violence, anger, sexual abuse, abortion, emotional abuse, mental disorders, anxiety disorder, eating disorders, mood disorders, parenting, conflict management, technology interference.

The Church needs to be able to minister to hurting people. The expected end-time harvest will usher people from all sorts of backgrounds who have found Christ and need to be mentored or discipled into knowing and living out their newfound faith, consistent with God's will for their lives. Part of the training must include informed awareness about the real-world issues people are suffering to avoid displaying shock, judgment, disapproval, or other harmful expressions.

Enlightening the Uninformed

Randy Newman, PhD, a Campus Crusade for Christ staff member, and adjunct professor of biblical studies at Patrick Henry College wrote an article titled "Evangelizing in a World Drowning in Sexual Problems." In the article he wrote:

> When people ask me what major lessons I learned while conducting interviews of new converts, my first thoughts go to

the reality of pain. Many of these students talked about struggles, hurts, and wounds. And most of those difficulties pointed to sex. This generation has a lot of sex, watches a lot of porn, experiences a horrific amount of abuse, and can't quite figure out how to think about this ever-present-but-seldom-joyous issue of sex.

Evangelism today occurs in a world that is drowning is sexual problems, misunderstandings, and a hardening against the gospel as a result.

During the sexual revolution of the 1960s, when people rebelled against the "traditional" view of sex (i.e., it was to occur only within lifelong, heterosexual marriage), people knew they were rebelling! They thought the old ways were constrictive, repressive, and boring. They saw their experiences as liberating, avant-garde, and revolutionary. But, somehow, they still considered their practices as non-normative.

Today's college students are so far removed from that time, they think their hooking up culture is the norm. They can't imagine why or how anyone would or could wait until marriage for sex. There's no reason they shouldn't take birth control pills, carry condoms, and know where to get an abortion if an "accident" should occur. The ones having sex on the first, second, or third dates (certainly no later than that!) think they are the norm and would feel guilty if they weren't in bed that early in a relationship.

And yet the painful expressions on their faces, the shameful tones in their voices, and their bewilderment at how such a "natural" act has delivered such pain haunts me even a year or more after concluding my face to face interviews.

123

How does this impact our evangelism efforts? Here are a few reflections, but I think the church needs to do a lot of brainstorming about ways to alter our pronouncement of the good news to an audience involved in, pressured by, and damaged by sex outside of God's parameters.[1]

His article offers a good deal of sensitivity training to help the Church better minister to those in need. More can be learned from his book, *Unlikely Converts: Improbable Stories of Faith and What They Teach Us About Evangelism* (Kregel Publications).

In taping my internet television programs, I met an amazing couple, Louis and Janey DeMeo from Harvest Alliance International. They spent twenty-two years in France where they founded a church, a Christian school, and a theological institute. They shared several stories about encounters they had while ministering in France. One I recall was their ministry to a large group of eunuchs in France. These individuals had been castrated, then, for various reasons, were no longer needed by the people they served. Unable to easily integrate with society, they formed a commune where they lived together. Louis and Janey spent time sharing the love of Jesus with these eunuchs and the entire community became believers in Jesus.

When they shared this story, I could not help but think, *Am I prepared to be sensitive and show Christ's love to people with life experiences far different than my own?* Learning more about the real-world pain and deceptions people suffer, I encourage church leadership to start now with sensitivity training not only with staff, but the congregation. When a "very different" person sits next to one of the congregation members, it is important the member is able to display nothing but a warm reception with Christ's love.

Vet Existing Ministries

God established the Church to operate in unity. He did not intend there to be competition and comparisons among Christians. The way I say it is, "Cooperation is heavenly, competition is worldly. One creates unity, the other creates division." It is my hope we can press far past the divisions and support one another. Your local church cannot possibly meet every need of every person who comes to you for help. Evaluate your church's strengths, then find ways to address the weaknesses. One excellent way is to vet existing parachurch organizations, then refer people to these when necessary.

Parachurch organizations are Christian faith-based organizations that usually carry out their mission independent of church oversight. It is easy to find lists on the internet. When vetting an organization, use a ranking service such as Guide Star as part of your process.

J. Mack Stiles, wrote an article, "Nine Marks of a Healthy Parachurch Ministry." In it he says:

> The standard cliché for parachurch is that it's not the church, but an arm of the church. Yet historically, that arm has shown a tendency to develop a mind of its own and crawl away from the body, which creates a mess. Given the grand scope and size of many parachurch ministries, those which go wayward can propagate error for years: missionary organizations become gyms, heretical seminaries pump out heretical pastors, and service organizations produce long-term confusion between the gospel and social action.
>
> So what should mark a healthy parachurch?
>
> Mark 1: A healthy parachurch ministry knows that it exists primarily to protect the church.

125

Mark 2: A healthy parachurch ministry makes a clear distinction between church and parachurch.

Mark 3: A healthy parachurch ministry avoids acting like the church.

Mark 4: A healthy parachurch ministry does not pressure the church to act like a parachurch.

Mark 5: A healthy parachurch ministry humbly heeds the history of parachurch movements.

Mark 6: A healthy parachurch ministry understands the difference between the pragmatic and the principled.

Mark 7: The healthy parachurch has a counter-cultural understanding of management and money.

Mark 8: The healthy parachurch maintains a strong commitment to, and understanding of, the gospel.

Mark 9: A healthy parachurch ministry seeks accountability relationships with the church.[2]

Stiles' article is quite good. I encourage you to read it to understand more about his nine marks to better help you partner with parachurch organizations. Many of Stiles' nine marks for a healthy parachurch organization are excellent marks local churches should seek to attain.

There are many excellent parachurch organizations local churches need to be aware of and maintain as resources to refer people to when the local church does not have the ability to help in a particular area of need. The following are most worthy of consideration:

- American Family Association
- Family Life Ministries
- Legal Defense Foundation

- Man in the Mirror
- Pure Life Ministries
- The Salvation Army.

The above list is an exceptionally small sampling of organizations that have earned excellent reputations. The Salvation Army is particularly noteworthy as they offer a variety services:

- adult rehabilitation
- veterans affairs services
- prison ministries
- elderly services
- combatting human trafficking
- missing persons
- hunger relief
- housing and homeless services
- Christmas assistance
- youth camps and recreation
- KROC centers
- emergency disaster services

If local churches learn what parachurch organizations and services are available in their community, we will be much better equipped to help people without over burdening church leadership by attempting to minister and meet needs where experience, qualifications, and resources are lacking. Again, why reinvent the wheel if God has already established a worthy ministry organization for you to partner with?

Research Available Resources

There are also excellent materials, such as books, DVDs and more, available to equip church leadership minister in difficult areas. Church leadership needs to equip and train men and women now to be able to minister to all kinds of human brokenness. Let the following list be a starting point for you to consider what your church needs, or where you may personally be called of God to minister.

This list is a small representation of brokenness where people need help. Filtering these topics down to know how to help people with specific needs is essential. Again, if your church cannot or would prefer not to minister in any given area, be sure to know of parachurch resources that can.

- domestic violence/abuse
- suicide
- bullying
- abortion
- sexual issues
- foster care
- marriage issues
- finances
- anger
- trauma
- addictions

Consider anonymously polling your congregation or other groups to see what needs exist within your community. Then prayerfully determine how to help.

Connect with Local Area Churches

One way to make Christianity more visible in your community is to hold events together with other local churches. This is an excellent way to display unity, while respecting our differences. In my own church, our lead pastor reached out to other churches in our community with 300 or fewer members. My pastor knows about the issues small churches face and knew by connecting and showing support one for another, they could fortify local pastors and increase the image of the Church in the community. It started with a half-day gathering including a catered lunch. At first there was suspicion about the agenda, but when it was clear that the only agenda was to connect in mutual support, the atmosphere radically changed. Now these half-day events are a regular occurrence.

The ideas of what local churches can do to bring the community together under the banner of Jesus, is sourced by creativity. Let the following list serve as a starting point for your creativity.

- Initiate a community service day with the city or county. Learn what community services your city/county needs. Then coordinate a date, get the word out and have volunteers from each church, sporting their own colored T-shirts get busy on the project. Cleaning up a public area that has been ill attended is one such project.
- Decide on a local pro-life charity, coordinate a day to walk and raise awareness and funds for the organization. Again, each church sporting their own T-shirts walking down major streets, waiving at cars and others along the way will do a lot for the image of the Church in your community.

129

- Partner with a well-respected service organization to hold a mini-fair for the underprivileged children, complete with simple games and prizes, jump houses and the like. Rally the contributions of local fast-food or food trucks to donate their menu items.

Learn what your community needs. Partner with local churches and organizations and visibly make a caring difference in your community.

In the next section, we will turn our focus to the essentials needed to prepare the atmosphere and the way for the harvest of souls.

PART THREE

HARVESTING SOULS

When he saw the crowds, he had compassion for them, because
they were harassed and helpless, like sheep without a shepherd.
Then he said to his disciples, "The harvest is plentiful, but the
laborers are few; therefore pray earnestly to the Lord of the
harvest to send out laborers into his harvest."

—Matthew 9:36–38

CHAPTER NINE

Possess Proper Fear of the Lord

The Bible is clear that evil increases and godly wisdom is lost when the fear of God is missing. To both nations and individuals God says through the prophet Jeremiah, "Your evil will chastise you, and your apostasy will reprove you. Know and see that it is evil and bitter for you to forsake the LORD your God; the fear of me is not in you, declares the LORD God of hosts."

Godless Culture

By simply observing headline news, it is clear that the fear of the Lord is not apparent in our American culture. An increase of lawlessness, violence, and crime, and the disrespect of authority in general are the order of the day. Sin increases where there is no fear of God. Psalm 36:1 says, "Transgression speaks to the wicked deep in his heart; there is no fear of God before his eyes." The absence of the fear of God is the natural outcome considering we have had several generations of students educated through the public school system that once revered Christianity and now teaches evolution as man's origin.

People are openly living in rebellion against God and are hostile toward Christians, believing us to be unenlightened, even deplorable. What should we expect? Those who are not-born again through faith in Christ, are simply living according to their naturally-born state. We are all naturally-born sinners, at enmity with God from birth. Aware of it or not, those who refuse to place their faith in God are actually cooperating with the plans of the Enemy. They are deceived about their condition, and the fact that they are on the path for eternal separation from God.

Ecclesiastes 8:11 says, "Because the sentence against an evil deed is not executed speedily, the heart of the children of man is fully set to do evil." Lawbreakers without immediate conviction or arrest consider themselves able to outsmart the law and continue to break more of God's laws.

Christian Responsibility

The increase of lawlessness and rejection of God is directly proportionate to the measure of Christian influence in the culture. This is why we need to understand that we as Christians have set ourselves up for judgment first. We need to take 1 Peter 4:17 very serious, "For it is time for judgment to begin at the household of God; and if it begins with us, what will be the outcome for those who do not obey the gospel of God?"

I have said for several years now. and claim this as my personally coined quote, "We have generations of people going to hell in a handbasket that has been woven by the Church."

Jesus commissioned His followers clearly when he said, "All authority in heaven and on earth has been given to me. Go therefore and make disciples of all nations, baptizing them in the name of the Father and of the Son and of the Holy Spirit, teaching them to observe all that I have commanded you. And behold, I am with you always, to the end of the age" (Matt. 28:18–20).

Early on in the ministry work I have embraced a prophetic word was spoken over me which stated in part, "You will be a strong asset to the Church." I pondered that for some time then sensed the Holy Spirit say I would be a missionary to the Church. I remember thinking how sad that the church in America needs missionaries. However, while Christianity in other countries flourishes and increases, here in America it is on the decline. It seems to me the Church in America does not possess a proper fear of God. This is why I am initiating the Come Back to God™ campaign, previously mentioned. The imparted vision for this campaign is not with a first focus on unbelievers, but believers. Only when Christians are on fire with their faith and demonstrate a proper fear of the Lord will we be in position to attract unbelievers to Christ.

Fear of the Lord for a believer is not fear of being cast into hell, but of hearing a rebuke from Jesus on the day of His visitation. Proverbs 16:6 instructs us, "By steadfast love and faithfulness iniquity is atoned for, and by the fear of the Lord one turns away from evil." The world of unbelievers needs to see what fear of the Lord looks like—they need Christians to demonstrate fear of the Lord. When we respond with a proper fear of the Lord, with demonstrations of moral effort, we will experience God's blessings and favor. We will express joy in the midst of heartache, hope in the midst of suffering, and in these ways, our genuine faith will attract unbelievers.

In Jack Wellman's "What Happens When the Fear of God is Missing?" he wrote:

> The Bible is clear that a fear of God suppresses evil, but what is
> the fear of God? It's a holy, reverential, deep, and abiding respect

and regard for the Holy, Holy, Holy Lord God Almighty, Who is altogether holy and in a perpetual state of perfection in every way . . . So a fear of God (and yes, fearing the wrath of God) is a healthy, godly means of avoiding sin.

Fear of the Lord is in our best interests and should motivate the sinner to flee to the cross, because, "we must all appear before the judgment seat of Christ, so that each one may receive what is due for what he has done in the body, whether good or evil. Therefore, knowing the fear of the Lord, we persuade others" (2 Cor. 5:11–12). Jude also connects evangelism with the fear of God, telling us to "have mercy on those who doubt; save others by snatching them out of the fire; to others show mercy with fear, hating even the garment stained by the flesh" (Jude 1:22–23). In these passages, God shows that we are to use the fear of God to rescue the perishing, which is a fear of God's judgment, but for others, showing others mercy with the fear of God. Paul wrote that it was by "the fear of the Lord [that] we persuade others." It's not that we wish unbelievers harm, but we are to tell them that they need the same righteousness that Jesus Christ has to stand before God (2 Cor. 5:21).

With no fear of God there is no godly wisdom, with no godly wisdom, there will be no wise choices, and the wisest choice you or anyone could ever make is to repent and put your trust in Christ. Matthew Henry wisely wrote, "Where no fear of God is, no good is to be expected," and that's just what the Scriptures teach. Jesus leaves you and me with only one of two choices: "Whoever believes in the Son has eternal life; whoever does not obey the Son shall not see life, but the wrath of God remains on him" (John 3:36). Complaining about the wrath of God is like

complaining that the ship is sinking while ignoring the lifeboats.
Just be glad there are lifeboats (John 3:16).[1]

Personal Audit

When we do not maintain a strong, spiritual communion with the Lord—
when we fail to feed on the full counsel of His Word, we begin accepting the
claims of the culture. We will be influenced by what popular and influential
people claim instead of what the Bible actually teaches. Unwittingly, we
compromise a little at a time and can eventually slip into sin—worldliness.
Before we know it, we are engaged in dark activities we never thought we
would be. Hebrew 2:1 admonishes us:

> We must pay much closer attention to what we have heard, lest
> we drift away from it. For since the message declared by angels
> proved to be reliable, and every transgression or disobedience
> received a just retribution, how shall we escape if we neglect such
> a great salvation? It was declared at first by the Lord, and it was
> attested to us by those who heard, while God also bore witness by
> signs and wonders and various miracles and by gifts of the Holy
> Spirit distributed according to his will.

Bert Farias addresses the importance of understanding God's judgment.
Using the apostle Paul's rebuke of the Corinthian church for tolerating sexual
immorality in their midst, Farias states lack of the fear of the Lord was the
reason. Chapter five of 1 Corinthians makes this clear.

> I have found that having this foundation of His judgments in your
> life is what cultivates the true fear of the Lord. Believers think it's

deep when you speak about the Lord's judgments, but it's actually one of the principle doctrines of Christ (Heb. 6:1–2). The Word calls it milk (Heb. 5:12–13). It's one of the first things new believers are supposed to learn. Yet it's a missing theme in most of the church. Why? Because we have substituted our own contemporary gospel for the gospel that Jesus and the apostles preached. As a result, the church is full of false converts. We avoid such themes as God's eternal judgments, holiness, repentance and the like. Too many casual and carnal believers actually think those themes are too negative and that they minister death and condemnation. But the Bible is full of warnings and exhortations such as the aforementioned that need to be emphasized, especially in this day of such moral degradation that is nearing collapse.[2]

What about you? As you evaluate yourself, do you have a proper fear of the Lord? What follows are some personal questions to help us honestly evaluate ourselves. As stated before, it is hard to be objective when you are the object. Pray asking the Holy Spirit to convict where conviction is needed. Remember the Holy Spirit is a loving administrator of justice. If we are not living with a proper fear of the Lord, and we do not assess ourselves, we position ourselves to be judged. It is better we seek to humble ourselves.

- Am I engaged in questionable activities the Lord would disapprove?
- Am I engaged in known sinful activities the Lord will judge?
- Do I communicate approval over sinful conditions in the life of fellow Christians by not lovingly addressing?
- Do I understand by not lovingly addressing sin in a fellow believer's life, I am accountable?

- What does my internet browsing, film, and television viewing history reveal about me?

- Are there things I do in secret that I would rather no one know about?

- Do I regularly entertain unwholesome thoughts and speak unwholesome words?

These are great starter questions to help you come up with more of your own.

The Holy Spirit is always the Spirit of holiness. He shows us our sin not to condemn us, but to show us where we have turned away from righteousness. The Holy Spirit seeks us to work with Him to become more holy.

True Holiness

There is a sinister silence from church leadership today on true holiness. This failure to provide instruction on the importance of holiness is causing many to fall back into sin and compromise the tenets of the Christian faith. As we have already explored, many born-again Christians have an apathetic attitude toward their faith and relationship with God. They are at best lukewarm, which is wholly unacceptable to God, as clearly expressed in Revelation 3:16.

The apostle Paul wrote in 2 Corinthians 7:1: "Since we have these promises, beloved, let us cleanse ourselves from every defilement of body and spirit, bringing holiness to completion in the fear of God."

To address the trend of the Church falling away from living holy lives I created a four-part retreat in 2002 titled "Journey into Holiness." I realized we had drifted so far we needed help to find our way back. One of the key verses for that message is Psalm 24:3–4: "Who shall ascend the hill of the Lord?

And who shall stand in his holy place? He who has clean hands and a pure heart, who does not lift up his soul to what is false and does not swear deceitfully."

And Luke 6:45 says: "The good person out of the good treasure of his heart produces good, and the evil person out of his evil treasure produces evil, for out of the abundance of the heart his mouth speaks."

God instructs us to be holy as He is holy (1 Peter 1:15). If we are children of God, we must cooperate with Him in the process of *sanctification*—we must be holy as He is holy. To be sanctified is to make holy; set apart as sacred; to be consecrated; to purify ourselves from sin. God's judgment is stricter on His children than unbelievers. This is why Philippians 2:12 admonishes us to "work our out own salvation with fear and trembling." Our salvation comes by first being convicted of the Lord about our sin, then willfully placing our faith in Christ to be justified from our sin. Next we need to learn how to live our new lives in Christ, which is the process of sanctification.

Here is another gleaning from Faris' article.

> The fear of the Lord is not a mere fear of His punishment for our disobedience, although that is a part of it, but a holy reverence and wholesome dread of displeasing Him. It is to be the controlling motive of the true Christian's life. It is the key component that perfects holiness in us. Holiness is an apostolic theme that runs through the entire New Testament and letters to the churches. How have we missed that?
>
> And what is it that nurtures the fear of the Lord in your life? It's the judgments of God or what is known as one of the 6 principles doctrines of Christ—eternal judgment. Repentance from dead works is another one of the doctrines of Christ. How

do we not emphasize that? Today repentance is somehow a dirty word, but it is a foundational doctrine.

Did you know that the judgment seat of Christ is also called the fear of the Lord?[3]

The Purpose of God's Judgment

God's judgments up until the Final Judgment are not meant to either condemn or justify. His judgments are meant to bring us into agreement with God through His truth and righteousness. Christ's righteousness is imputed to born-again Christians as a gift from God. For us to fail to cooperate with Him in the process of sanctification is an exceedingly high insult to Christ who suffered in our place so we can be made righteous.

Farias explains further.

> God is raising up judges (ministers who preach the whole counsel of God) in this hour to bring the people of God into true union with Him. Our nation is under judgment for this very reason. But judgment begins in the house of God with teachers and all ministers receiving the stricter end of it (James 3:1).
>
> Read Romans 1. See what happens to a people who suppress the truth in unrighteousness (v. 18). God eventually gives them over to uncleanness, vile passions, and a debased mind (v. 24, 26, and 28). You might object and say, "These verses are speaking of homosexuality!" But notice v. 32 "Who, knowing the righteous judgment of God, that those who practice such things are deserving of death, not only do the same but also approve of those who practice them."

When you vote for public officials who approve of same sex marriage you are operating with no judgment out of a debased mind.

The Church is in a mess today because she does not know Jesus as the Lord and Judge. "Lord" is a word we say, but it does not mean Supreme Ruler over our lives. "Judge" is a word we avoid because we think it's not love, and we defend it with our "thou-shalt-not-judge" mantra. But Jesus is the righteous Judge, and the Father has committed all judgment to Him.

"For the Father judges no one, but has committed all judgment to the Son" (John 5:22).

You cannot come into agreement with God unless you know His ways and His heart—both His goodness and severity, His love and holiness, His mercy and judgment. There is a present level of deception today mostly because we are not familiar with His judgments. I believe that walking in the light of God's Word and His judgments is the greatest present need in the body of Christ in this hour. [4]

The next chapter will help us better grasp the tremendous transformation God intends our faith in Christ to produce.

CHAPTER TEN

Embrace New Identity

As I wrote in the Introduction, the Enemy's lies have successfully caused many people to be deceived. Many think they are born-again Christians when their character and lifestyles say otherwise. This is the worst possible reality for these precious people.

As I shared, I lived that way for the first nearly thirty years of my life. I had said a prayer as a little girl, just as the Sunday school teacher suggested. Based on the teacher's instructions, I thought I was a Christian. It was not until I experienced a major life crisis that I learned my faith was not intact. I thought when I died I would go to heaven because of the prayer asking Jesus to be my Savior. I later learned that the offer Jesus makes to us requires we place our faith in Him as both Savior and Lord. I wanted Jesus to be my savior as an insurance policy to keep me from going to hell. But I had been lord of my own life in every way, which is why it became such a mess.

Once I wholly surrendered my will to God's will for my life, I was spiritually transformed into a new being that had never before existed. It is the same for all who genuinely surrender to God through faith in Jesus, according to 2 Corinthians 5:17.

Deception Regarding Salvation

Many people today approach their faith in Jesus the same way I originally did. They want Jesus to prevent them from eternal damnation, but live their lives exactly as they please with no regard, and in some cases no knowledge, of God's standards for daily life. This category of "Christians" are *namesake only*.

I am a perfect example. I called myself Christian and believed I was a Christian because of a prayer I uttered. However, my lifestyle clearly showed I merely claimed to be Christian. I did not fully know what it is to be a genuine Christian.

It is wise for those who say they are saved to examine their life and their walk asking if it is in line with the biblical doctrine of salvation. This is a matter of eternal life or death. To know if this is you or not, ask yourself "Who is truly Lord of my life?" If you live with primary focus on pleasing yourself, you are lord of your life. Conversely, if your primary focus is to please God, then He is Lord of your life.

Namesake only is one category of salvation deceptions. In George Barna's book, *The Seven Faith Tribes: Who They Are, What They Believe, and Why They Matter,* published in 2009, he identifies seven faith sectors. He refers to each sector as a tribe. His research revealed Casual Christians represent 66 percent of the adult population of the U.S. The percentage of the adult population represented by the other half-dozen tribes included 16 percent who are Captive Christians, 2 percent Jews, 2 percent Mormons, 2 percent pantheists, one-half of 1 percent Muslims, and 11 percent skeptics.

Barna's book was published before much research had been gained concerning millennials. With the Pew Study "Religion Among Millennials"[1] we learn one in four members of the millennial generation are unaffiliated with any particular faith. Millennials make up nearly a quarter of the population of the United States today.

The two Christian groups, Casual and Captive Christians are distinctly different. Casual Christians are born-again, but their regard for God's instructions for daily living is selective. Casual Christians have also been referred to as Carnal Christians for the reasons Barna provides:

> Casual Christianity is faith in moderation. It allows them to feel religious without having to prioritize their faith. Christianity is a low-risk, predictable proposition for this tribe, providing a faith perspective that is not demanding. A Casual Christian can be all the things that they esteem: a nice human being, a family person, religious, an exemplary citizen, a reliable employee, and never have to publicly defend or represent difficult moral or social positions or even lose much sleep over their private choices as long as they mean well and generally do their best. From their perspective, their brand of faith practice is genuine, realistic and practical. To them, Casual Christianity is the best of all worlds; it encourages them to be a better person than if they had been irreligious, yet it is not a faith into which they feel compelled to heavily invest themselves.
>
> [The appeal for Casual Christians is] the comfort that this approach provides. It offers them life insights if they choose to accept them, gives them a community of relationships if they desire such, fulfills their inner need to have some type of connection with a deity, and provides the image of being a decent, faith-friendly person. Because Casuals do not view matters of faith as central to one's purpose or success in life, this brand of Christianity supplies the multi-faceted levels of satisfaction and

assurance that they desire. Casual Christians are defined by the desire to please God, family, and other people while extracting as much enjoyment and comfort from the world as possible. For Casuals, success is balancing everything just right so that they are able to maximize their opportunities and joys in life without undermining their perceived relationship with God and others. [2]

While Casual Christians are considered middle-of-the-road, even ambivalent about their faith, they are an important sector of American Christians. Casual Christians are comprised of significant proportions of minimally active and moderately active born-again Christians. At the same time they are theologically nominal Christians. Many in this group are biblically illiterate or minimally familiar with Scripture. Yet Barna believes:

> If a catalyst were added to this mix to deepen this tribe's integration of faith and lifestyle, or even to simply create more extensive sense of community and purpose within the tribe, unprecedented changes [in culture and society] could occur.[3]

The other category of Christians according to Barna, is Captive Christians. These are born-again believers that Barna describes as follows:

> Captive Christians are focused on upholding the absolute moral and spiritual truths they glean from the Bible. The lives of Captive Christians are defined by their faith; their worldview is built around their core spiritual beliefs and resultant values. For Captives, success is obedience to God, as demonstrated by consistently serving Christ and carrying out His commands and principles [in everyday life].

Answering the question, "Is Casual Christianity bad for America?" Barna replied:

> That, of course, depends on your point of view. Several of the non-Christian tribes consider all Christians to be heretics or at least spiritually misguided. Captive Christians consider Casuals to not be genuine followers of Christ. In terms of the future of the republic, there is something to be said for people who are willing to compromise for the good of the whole community, but there are also difficulties raised when people do not stand for anything or cannot identify the truths that are worth championing. From a spiritual vantage point, that is especially important if moral and spiritual truths are all considered to be relative. Casual Christianity, because of its moral receptivity and pliability, generally eliminates spiritual backbone from moral discussions. And yet, Casual Christians would typically embrace the twenty shared values that all seven of the tribes adopt as part of their moral code.[4]

Where do you see yourself in these descriptions? Where do you see most of the people in your congregation? How would you define the early Christians—do you see them as Casual or Captive Christians? I would think we would have to agree they were Captive Christians.

Whether you are a non-Christian, skeptic, Casual or Captive Christian, there is always the option to identify any deceptive mindset we have and exchange it for an increased knowledge of truth. It is, as stated, an option. Not all people want to change their comfortable lifestyle. However, if people would take Scripture concerning judgment and reward for the serious reality it is, the desire to change for the better as a Christian should be embraced. Consider the following Scriptures:

> But because of your hard and impenitent heart you are storing up wrath for yourself on the day of wrath when God's righteous judgment will be revealed. He will render to each one according to his works: 7 to those who by patience in well-doing seek for glory and honor and immortality, he will give eternal life; 8 but for those who are self-seeking[a] and do not obey the truth, but obey unrighteousness, there will be wrath and fury.
>
> (Rom. 2:5–8)

> Therefore do not pronounce judgment before the time, before the Lord comes, who will bring to light the things now hidden in darkness and will disclose the purposes of the heart. Then each one will receive his commendation from God.
>
> (1 Cor. 4:5)

> So whether we are at home or away, we make it our aim to please him. For we must all appear before the judgment seat of Christ, so that each one may receive what is due for what he has done in the body, whether good or evil.
>
> (2 Cor. 5:9–10)

God Longs to Reward Us

As our Creator and loving Father, God wants only the best for us. He proved that through His Son, who was the substitutionary sacrifice to atone for sin for all who will place their faith in Jesus. Scripture reveals God created us for good works. He has deposited within each of us our own unique set of talents, gifts, and interests to guide us into His perfect calling and purpose for our life. The work He wants us to do is to bring His Kingdom will to be done on earth as it is in heaven. God's focus is to utterly transform the earth and the heavens into a new earth and heaven where evil will no longer have any influence.

The deeds we do in this natural life determine the quality of relationship we have with God and others, and also determines our eternal reward. I especially like Hebrews 11:6 that says, "And without faith it is impossible to please him, for whoever would draw near to God must believe that he exists and that he rewards those who seek him." Placing our faith in Jesus positions us for eternal life and eternal reward.

We have been born to partner with God to transform the world. The deeds we do in Christ actually impact the spiritual world to bring transformation to the natural world. All this reminds me of two parables Jesus told His disciples concerning His return and our reward.

Parable of the Ten Virgins

Then the kingdom of heaven will be like ten virgins who took their lamps and went to meet the bridegroom. Five of them were foolish, and five were wise. For when the foolish took their lamps, they took no oil with them, but the wise took flasks of oil with their lamps. As the bridegroom was delayed, they all became drowsy and slept. But at midnight there was a cry, 'Here is the bridegroom! Come out to meet him.' Then all those virgins rose and trimmed their lamps. And the foolish said to the wise, 'Give us some of your oil, for our lamps are going out.' But the wise answered, saying, 'Since there will not be enough for us and for you, go rather to the dealers and buy for yourselves.' And while they were going to buy, the bridegroom came, and those who were ready went in with him to the marriage feast, and the door was shut. Afterward the other virgins came also, saying, 'Lord, lord, open to us.' But he answered, 'Truly, I say to you, I do not know you.' Watch therefore, for you know neither the day no the hour.

(Matt. 25: 1–13)

Parable of the Talents

For it will be like a man going on a journey, who called his servant and entrusted to them his property. To one he gave five talents, to another two, to another one, to each according to his ability. Then he went away. He who had received the five talents went at once and traded with them, and he made five talents more. So also he who had the two talents made two talents more. But he who had received the one talent went and dug in the ground and hid his master's money. Now after a long time the master of those servants came and settled accounts with them. And he who had received the five talents came forward, bringing five talents more, saying, 'Master, you delivered to me five talents; here, I have made five talents more.' His master said to him, 'Well done, good and faithful servant. You have been faithful over a little; I will set you over much. Enter into the joy of your master.' And he also who had the two talents came forward, saying, 'Master, you delivered to me two talents; here, I have made two talents more.' His master said to him, 'Well done, good and faithful servant. You have been faithful over a little; I will set you over much. Enter into the joy of your master.' He also who had received the one talent came forward, saying, 'Master, I knew you to be a hard man, reaping where you did not sow, and gathering where you scattered no seed, so I was afraid, and I went and hid your talent in the ground. Here, you have what is yours.' But his master answered him, 'You wicked and slothful servant! You knew that I reap where I have not sown and gather where I scattered no seed? Then you ought to have invested my money with the bankers, and at my coming I should have received what was my own with interest. So take the talent from him and give it to him who has the ten talents. For to everyone who has will more be given, and he will have an abundance. But from the one who has not, even what he has will be taken away. And cast the worthless servant into the outer darkness. In that place there will be weeping and gnashing of teeth.

(Matt. 25:14–30)

Immediately after telling these two parables, Jesus explains what the final judgment will be like. You can read this in Matthew 25:31–46.

You may be completely familiar with the passages above. You may read them here and find yourself considering them in a new way. You may be a Christian leader who realizes the importance of ensuring your congregation is properly taught the realities of being a non-believer, Casual Christian or Captive Christian. As explored earlier in this book, God is an all-in God. He wants us to be all-in Christians. My catch phrase and sign-off on radio and television is, "Remember, Christ died for us; the least we can do is live for Him."

Our New Identity in Christ

When we place our faith in Jesus as Savior and Lord, we spiritually become entirely new creatures in Christ. With this new spirit, and the indwelling of the Holy Spirit, we are justified, atoned by the blood of Jesus. Many say to be justified is "just as if I never sinned." Let me clarify. Born-again Christians are justified the moment they place their faith in Christ. With the indwelling of the Holy Spirit, and a new spirit, sanctification comes after justification. This is the process of instructing and directing our soul, mind, and body how to live our new life in Christ.

One of the most important things we need in this present abhorrent culture is to deeply know who we are in Christ, and not allow the Enemy of God to whisper lies causing us to consider ourselves disqualified. We are who God says we are. If more Christians would actively meditate and own who God says we are in Christ, the authority and power of Jesus would swiftly change the culture for the better.

I recently spoke before a group of Christians, challenging them to be all-in Christians. The message was called, "You Are Who God Says You Are— Receive It, Believe It, Demonstrate It." I provided a list of seventy-six passages in the Bible where God makes a clear and positive affirmation of who we are in Christ. You'll find it in the appendix of this book. I encourage you to read these passages, meditate on them, and get them fixed deeply in your conviction about yourself. Then observe how you are transformed more and more, and notice the impact you will have on everyone and everything around you. This is the evidence of transformation from sanctification.

New Identity, New Intimacy

As we come to a much more clear understanding of who God says we are as Christians, we find ourselves falling deeper and deeper in love with God. Then we are able to better comprehend the depth of love God has for us individually. God's love and presence is always available for us. He initiates; we respond only according to what we believe. Again, it is highly possible for Christians to be deceived on different matters. It is the tactic of the Enemy.

He knows once we understand our true identity in Christ, and fully embrace and experience God's love, we are transformed beyond his ability to deceive us. When we come to this place in our faith-walk, we have all the confidence and humility needed for God to work in and through us, further defeating the Enemy.

When Christians come to this place in their life in Christ, they exude the love and power of Christ. When we read about Jesus' early disciples doing miraculous works as He did, we are observing Christians who are all-in.

John 14:12 records the words of Jesus to His disciples: "Truly, truly I say to you, whoever believes in me will also do the works that I do; and greater works than these will he do, because I am going to the Father." In John chapter 17 Jesus prays for His disciples, not just those within His hearing, but those who are yet to exist. That includes all Christians since Christ's ascension—including you and me. In John 17:11 and 17:21, Jesus prays for His disciples left in the world, asking the Father to keep us in His name that we may be one even as Jesus and the Father are one, so the world may believe that the Father sent Jesus.

God's challenge to the Church today is to be all-in—to willingly cooperate with His process of sanctification. If we resist, we can expect to be corrected by God's discipline. No discipline is pleasant in the moment, but it produces the needed correction.

We have taken a good look at the dreadful condition of the Church in America. We know the chaos, conflict, and destruction rampant in our culture. Our response must be to fully understand the solution to all that is evil and perverse is for God's people to rise up and take their rightful place in God's plan.

Once we evaluate ourselves and rededicate ourselves to God, He will lovingly and without condemnation guide us further in the transformation process. Based on many trusted prophetic words and my own understanding of the time we are living in, we can expect a swift work of God in transforming us. The Church has squandered precious time and opportunities. But God will make up for lost impact and give recompense to the Enemy as we commit ourselves to Christ and rise up to our calling.

CHAPTER ELEVEN

Become Christ's Disciples

Before we can participate with Jesus' instruction to make disciples of all nations (Matt. 28:18–20), we need to make certain we ourselves are practicing disciples of Christ. We need to possess a proper foundation of understanding of our Christian faith and who we are in Christ. The previous chapters have been devoted to helping us gain an honest evaluation of ourselves as individuals and collectively as the Church. Here we will proceed to be certain our understanding and response to our faith is accurate.

Religion vs. Relationship

One area with a considerable amount of confusion is understanding the difference between religion and relationship—or as I often say, the difference between performance and preference. Performance includes acts or works we do out of our own ability, in a religious fashion. Preference is the genuine, considered desire to have relationship with God, understanding His love has nothing to do with performance. Performance is an act of the will. Preference is a desire of the heart. It is my hope that in preparation for the expected great harvest of souls, Christians and church leadership will emphasize a proper understanding of our relationship with God through faith in Christ.

What we have succumbed to over many decades is the wrong understanding that we can earn God's love. The Bible is clear in several places that there is nothing we can do to earn God's love. Romans 5:8 says, "God shows his love for us in that while we were still sinners, Christ died for us."

Knowing the love of God for us is essential for effective Christian faith. God's love is fundamental to our identity as His children, and as brothers and sisters with one another through faith in Christ. By faith in Jesus' sacrifice, the supreme demonstration of God's love, we are welcomed into the family of God. Jesus has done everything needed for us to enter into loving relationship with God and one another.

Certain denominational churches teach a doctrine of "works" that they believe is necessary to remain in God's love. Pastor Josh Lotzenhiser's testimony in Chapter Six is one example of the performance doctrine. This doctrine is actually a tactic of the Enemy intended to defeat us. No one can live a perfect life at all times, except Jesus. By God's grace expressed toward us in the life, death, and resurrection of Jesus we are offered salvation. It is God's grace and nothing we can ever do that allows us to enter into His love, so no man can boast.

Romans 8:37–39 says:

> No, in all these things [sufferings and persecutions in this life] we are more than conquerors through him who loved us. For I am sure that neither death nor life, nor angels nor rulers, nor things present nor things to come, nor powers, nor height nor depth, nor anything else in all creation, will be able to separate us from the love of God in Christ Jesus our Lord.

God's Love and Approval

As I learned from one of my mentors, Rich Buhler, who is home with the Lord, is the fact that love and approval are two separate matters. Unfortunately, some earthly parents will create an atmosphere that makes the child feel unloved when they disapprove of their child's behavior. This makes the parent's love conditional based on the child's performance. This human perspective about love demonstrated in many families is then translated to an incorrect human belief about God's love.

In reality, God's love is unconditional. However, on the other hand, His approval is conditional. Love and approval are two distinct matters. The many instructions for godly living found in the Bible (God's Word) are entirely given for us to experience the best possible human existence. God is the Creator of all humanity and as Creator He knows what is best for us. Like the Old Testament nation of Israel did when they chose to embrace God's ways, we express our love to Him by our obedience. In return we experience the best possible life on earth as we live according to His will.

The Enemy of God has sought to prevent us from living in God's will beginning with the very first man and woman created. Satan knows every person he prevents from entering into relationship with God is destroying another of God's children made in His image. If the Enemy is not successful in preventing us from discovering the truth of Jesus allowing us to enter into right relationship with God, then the next best thing for him is to deceive us about God's character, will, and intent. To protect ourselves from any perverted understanding about God, we need to be personally familiar with His Word—the Bible. Then any teaching or influence to the contrary of God's Word can be confidently identified as false—as lies we will not accept.

God's Grace

Without God's grace we would have no hope—we would forever be doomed to hell, separated from God and all that is good. Every good thing we enjoy is because of the grace of God. Our salvation, our blessings, our successes—nothing good would be possible for us without God's grace.

Justin Holcomb, priest, teacher, and author wrote an article about God's Grace, shared in part here:

> Grace is most needed and best understood in the midst of sin, suffering, and brokenness. We live in a world of earning, deserving, and merit, and these result in judgment. That is why everyone wants and needs grace. Judgment kills. Only grace makes alive.
>
> A shorthand for what grace is —"mercy, not merit." Grace is the opposite of karma, which is all about getting what you deserve. Grace is getting what you don't deserve, and not getting what you do deserve. Christianity teaches that what we deserve is death with no hope of resurrection.
>
> While everyone desperately needs it, grace is not about us. Grace is fundamentally a word about God: His un-coerced initiative and pervasive, extravagant demonstrations of care and favor. Michael Horton writes, "In grace, God gives nothing less than Himself. Grace, then, is not a third thing or substance mediating between God and sinners, but is Jesus Christ in redeeming action."
>
> Christians live every day by the grace of God. We receive forgiveness according to the riches of God's grace, and grace drives our sanctification. Paul tells us, "the grace of God has

appeared, bringing salvation for all people, training us to renounce ungodliness and worldly passions, and to live self-controlled, upright, and godly lives" (Titus 2:11). Spiritual growth doesn't happen overnight; we "grow in the grace and knowledge of our Lord and Savior Jesus Christ" (2 Peter 2:18). Grace transforms our desires, motivations, and behavior.

In fact, God's grace grounds and empowers everything in the Christian life.[1]

With a proper understanding of God's grace, we must realize what a dangerous matter it is to *presume upon God's grace*. Many born-again Christians continue to live their lives while allowing sin to remain. Some are unaware of God's instructions; some have denied God's instructions. Either way, ignorant or willful, sin is sin and is cause for God to withdraw His approval. The apostle Paul dealt with believers who were indulging in sin as we read in Romans 5:20–6:4:

> Now the law came in to increase the trespass, but where sin increased, grace abounded all the more, so that, as sin reigned in death, grace also might reign through righteousness leading to eternal life through Jesus Christ our Lord.
>
> What shall we say then? Are we to continue in sin that grace may abound? By no means! How can we who died to sin still live in it? Do you not know that all of us who have been baptized into Christ Jesus were baptized into his death? We were buried therefore with him by baptism into death, in order that, just as Christ was raised from the dead by the glory of the Father, we too might walk in newness of life.

Faith in Jesus allows us to be spiritually born-again, re-created into an entirely new creature. Next, we are to follow in the process of sanctification so all of us, body, soul and spirit, can be renewed. However, this is where many Christians fall short, and are led more by their lusts of the flesh, than their love of God. Presuming upon God's grace is dangerous and sets us up for remedial judgment. When discipline is not swift the guilty continue in their ways, mounting up the loss of quality of life on earth and loss of eternal rewards.

It takes time and effort to move from being born-again to cooperating with the transforming power of the Holy Spirit. However, I can testify it is far better to actively cooperate than to intentionally sin.

God's Promises

God's love is unconditional, but many of His promises are not. For example, God's promise for Christ to return is unconditional. It is going to occur regardless of our reaction to the promise. Prophetic words from God are often unconditional promises of what is yet to come. God's promise of salvation, however, is conditional. It requires us to respond as God has determined in order to receive the promise. Many of God's promises are actually *offers* we can benefit from by responding as He has determined. Many times prophetic words in the Old Testament were given with an offer extended by God for what His people could do to avoid or lessen the punishment.

We need to know God's promises and what is required of us to benefit from His promises. Many Christians are ignorant of God's instruction about sin and thereby place themselves in line for discipline. Additionally, many Christians are ignorant about God's promises and therefore fail to benefit from them.

Being a disciple of Christ is an ongoing relationship of learning about God and His ways and becoming obedient. When we choose to be obedient (not perfect in performance but intentional about preference) we position ourselves to be blessed. We position ourselves to receive the best of all God longs to lavish upon us. Obedience is the visual demonstration of our heart condition. One definition of the Greek word for obedience in the New Testament is "to trust." Biblical obedience is to hear, trust, submit, and surrender to God and His Word. This is yet another aspect of the Christian faith I hope Christian leaders will emphasize to their congregations.

Mary Fairchild offers eight reasons why obedience to God is important. The following is a summary of the original article, which I recommend you read.

1. Jesus Calls Us to Obedience

In Jesus Christ we find the perfect model of obedience. As his disciples, we follow Christ's example as well as his commands. Our motivation for obedience is love:

If you love me, you will keep my commandments. (John 14:15, ESV)

2. Obedience Is an Act of Worship

While the Bible places strong emphasis on obedience, it's critical to remember that believers are not justified (made righteous) by our obedience. Salvation is a free gift of God, and we can do nothing to merit it. True Christian obedience flows from a heart of gratitude for the grace we have received from the Lord:

And so, dear brothers and sisters, I plead with you to give your bodies to God because of all he has done for you. Let them be a living and holy sacrifice—the kind he will find acceptable. This is truly the way to worship him. (Romans 12:1, NLT)

3. God Rewards Obedience

Over and over again we read in the Bible that God blesses and rewards obedience:

"And through your descendants all the nations of the earth will be blessed—all because you have obeyed me." (Genesis 22:18, NLT)

Jesus replied, "But even more blessed are all who hear the word of God and put it into practice." (Luke 11:28, NLT)

4. Obedience to God Proves Our Love

The books of 1 John and 2 John clearly explain that obedience to God demonstrates love for God. Loving God implies following his commands:

By this we know that we love the children of God, when we love God and obey his commandments. For this is the love of God, that we keep his commandments. (1 John 5:2–3, ESV)

Love means doing what God has commanded us, and he has commanded us to love one another, just as you heard from the beginning. (2 John 6, NLT)

5. Obedience to God Demonstrates Our Faith

When we obey God, we show our trust and faith in him:

"And we can be sure that we know him if we obey his commandments. If someone claims, "I know God," but doesn't obey God's commandments, that person is a liar and is not living in the truth. But those who obey God's word truly show how completely they love him. That is how we know we are living in him. Those who say they live in God should live their lives as Jesus did." (1 John 2:3–6, NLT)

6. Obedience is Better Than Sacrifice

The phrase "obedience is better than sacrifice," has often perplexed Christians. It can only be understood from an Old

Testament perspective. The law required the Israelite people to offer sacrifices to God, but those sacrifices and offerings were never intended to take the place of obedience. [See 1 Samuel 15:22-23]

7. Disobedience Leads to Sin and Death

The disobedience of Adam brought sin and death into the world. This is the basis of the term "original sin." But Christ's perfect obedience restores fellowship with God for everyone who believes in him:

For as by the one man's [Adam's] disobedience the many were made sinners, so by the one man's [Christ's] obedience the many will be made righteous. (Romans 5:19, ESV)

8. Through Obedience, We Experience the Blessings of Holy Living

Only Jesus Christ is perfect, therefore, only he could walk in sinless, perfect obedience. But as we allow the Holy Spirit to transform us from within, we grow in holiness. This is known as the process of sanctification, which can also be described as spiritual growth. The more we read God's Word, spend time with Jesus, and allow the Holy Spirit to change us from within, the more we grow in obedience and holiness as Christians. [See Psalms 119:1-8; Isaiah 48:17–19, and Corinthians 7:1.

We don't learn obedience overnight; it's a lifelong process that we pursue by making it a daily goal.[2]

Hearing God

In order to obey God, we must be able to "hear" Him. God speaks to us continually and in many different ways. He speaks through His written Word (logos word) the Bible, through creation, music, prayer, meditation, other people, circumstances, and directly by His Spirit to our spirit (rhema word), directly or through another Christian.

All genuine Christians hear God's voice. Many do not confidently recognize what they are hearing is actually God's voice. Consider radio and television stations. They transmit communication signals twenty-four days a week, seven days a week. We only connect with the communication when we turn our receiver on. Failure to connect with the signals does not mean the station is not transmitting. It is the same with God. God is constantly transmitting His voice to His sheep, but few have their receivers on. Most Christians are busy pleading with God in prayer asking to for Him to speak or transmit, when the problem is with their receivers. To upgrade our receivers we need to confidently know and have faith in what the Bible says about hearing God, quicken our ability to discern, and respond with obedience.

Psalm 46:10 starts with: "Be still, and know that I am God." This has two parts: to be still and to know. We need to learn to quiet our minds from all the distractions of life, and focus on God—focus on God's character, will, and intentions as revealed in the Bible to be confident (know) about Him.

To enter into time of intimate, conversational prayer, finding a quiet place, perhaps with worship music, and intentionally focus on God. I like to start with praise and adoration, then present my request, whatever it is. I do this typing at my computer. When I have said all I want to say, then I convert the font to italics and quietly wait on the Lord. Then I write down whatever comes to me without editing it, believing it is from the Lord.

I was at first dismissive when I heard nothing but lavish, loving words spoken to me. But I realized I would not say such wonderful things about myself, so I trusted it was the voice of God. Any words that are condemning are not from God. They are from the Enemy and are to be immediately tuned out. At the same time, God can be stern in speaking to us, especially at times of giving a warning. If heeding the warning would protect us, then it is from God. If heeding the "warning" would lead to hardship, loss, or suffering, it is not the voice of God. God wants only what is best for us. That does not mean we will avoid hardships, simply that God will not instruct us to do anything harmful.

John 4:24 says, "God is spirit, and those who worship him must worship in spirit and truth." God is spirit and we communicate directly with Him by our spirits, through prayer. The Lord speaks to our spirits not in words but in thoughts and impressions that we should then prayerfully put to words. Then we should meditate on what God has said, asking Him for any deeper insight, wisdom, or direction.

God's voice often sounds like what we hear when we are considering our own thoughts. But the nature of the words are different enough that we soon learn to trust we are hearing God's voice.

Psalm 37:4 reads: "Delight yourself in the Lord, and he will give you the desires of your heart." Some have wrongly interpreted this to mean God will grant any desire you have, even using this verse to justify selfishness, lust, greed, and so on. But God's Word is clear such are attitudes we are to lay down. He would not give us something inconsistent with His will for how we are to live. This verse actually means when we seek Him, He puts His desires into our hearts so our hearts line up with His will. In this way, when we pray from our hearts we are confident we are praying His will, and can expectantly wait for His answer to our prayers. Receiving His desires into our hearts is part of the process of sanctification.

Andrew Womack, a well-respected church leader shared about a time when he heard God's voice, but he did not trust it was God:

All the elders of the church were custom combiners. Six months of the year, they were gone following the wheat harvest. They insisted that we ordain another elder who would always be there. Their choice for eldership, I had nothing against, but as I prayed about this man and his wife, I didn't feel right ordaining him as an elder. However, being a man, I went with logic instead of my heart.

Within two weeks of the others leaving for wheat harvest, this new elder turned into the devil himself. In his reports to the elders, he accused me of stealing money from the church, committing adultery, drinking, smoking, and everything else you can imagine. It was a terrible experience. As soon as this man showed his true colors, I knew in my heart that the feelings and thoughts I had were the Lord speaking to me, and I had dismissed them as my own. I made a decision right then and there that I would never ignore my heart again.[3]

In another instance, Womack describes a time when God changed the desire of his heart and he obeyed:

I once was planning a trip to Costa Rica, a place I had been before, and was excited to be returning to. Yet, as I prayed about it, I lost my desire to go. Instead, I actually felt dread about going. The first thing I did when that happened was make sure I was really seeking the Lord with my whole heart. While on a road trip, I spent seventeen hours praying in tongues, and the more I got my mind stayed on the Lord, the less I wanted to go back to Costa Rica. On the strength of that alone, I canceled the trip.

When the people of Costa Rica asked why, all I could tell them was I didn't want to go. That was hard to do, and I'm not sure they understood. The plane I had booked my flight on crashed on take-off from Mexico City, killing all 169 persons onboard. The Lord warned me of that and saved my life, not by saying, "Don't go to Costa Rica," but by communicating to my spirit and taking away my desire to go. That is the dominant way the Lord speaks to us, and we often miss that kind of communication.[4]

In another example of God speaking and Womack hearing, Womack shares:

> One of the most important decisions of my life came in 1968. I was in college when the Lord radically touched my life, and all my desires changed. I didn't want to be in college anymore, and following those new desires, I made the decision to quit school. Then all hell broke loose. My mother didn't understand, and she quit talking to me for a time. Leaders in my church told me I was hearing from the devil. I stood to lose $350 per month in government support from my father's social security, and I would lose my student deferment from the draft. Without the deferment, I stood a good chance of ending up in Vietnam.
>
> Because of these adverse reactions to my decision, I backed off for a while and was absolutely miserable. This continued for two months until I couldn't take it anymore, and one night the Lord finally spoke to me through Romans 14:23, which says, "Whatsoever is not of faith is sin."
>
> I realized I was in sin because of indecision. I determined to make a faith decision that night and stick with it. As I prayed and

studied the Word for guidance, I found Colossians 3:15, which says, "And let the peace of God rule in your hearts."

The Lord spoke to me that I was to head in the direction that gave me the most peace. To be truthful, I didn't have total peace in any direction, but just as an umpire has to make a decision and stick with it, I needed to make the call. I had the most peace about quitting school, so I made the call and stepped out of indecision into faith, to the best of my understanding. Within twenty-four hours the Lord gave me such confirmation and joy that I have never doubted the wisdom of that decision since. That one decision, possibly more than any other, set my life on a course that has brought me to where I am today.[5]

Good earthly fathers want to maintain open communication with their children so they can be available to provide wisdom and counsel any time their children inquire. If human fathers want this type relationship, how much more does God, our Creator and heavenly Father?

Become Christ's Disciples

To be a genuine and continually growing disciple of Christ is to trust that God is exactly who He says He is, and you are exactly who He says you are. Jesus' prayer for all who belong to Him in the gospel of John is one of the most moving sections of the New Testament. All Christians need to read and deposit these passages deeply within their hearts. Confidently possessing this knowledge will allow you to dig deep and be fortified any time you encounter opposition. This chapter is often called "The High Priestly Prayer:"

When Jesus had spoken these words, he lifted up his eyes to heaven, and said, "Father, the hour has come; glorify your Son that the Son may glorify you, since you have given him authority over all flesh, to give eternal life to all whom you have given him. And this is eternal life, that they know you, the only true God, and Jesus Christ whom you have sent. I glorified you on earth, having accomplished the work that you gave me to do. And now, Father, glorify me in your own presence with the glory that I had with you before the world existed.

I have manifested your name to the people whom you gave me out of the world. Yours they were, and you gave them to me, and they have kept your word. Now they know that everything that you have given me is from you. For I have given them the words that you gave me, and they have received them and have come to know in truth that I came from you; and they have believed that you sent me. I am praying for them. I am not praying for the world but for those whom you have given me, for they are yours. All mine are yours, and yours are mine, and I am glorified in them. And I am no longer in the world, but they are in the world, and I am coming to you. Holy Father, keep them in your name, which you have given me, that they may be one, even as we are one. While I was with them, I kept them in your name, which you have given me. I have guarded them, and not one of them has been lost except the son of destruction, that the Scripture might be fulfilled. But now I am coming to you, and these things I speak in the world, that they may have my joy fulfilled in themselves. I have given them your word, and the world has hated them because they are not of the world, just as I am not of the world. I do not ask that you take them out of the world, but that you keep them from the evil one. They are not of the world, just as I am not of the world. Sanctify them[b] in the truth; your word is truth. As you sent me into the world, so I have sent them into the world. And for their sake I consecrate myself, that they also may be sanctified in truth.

I do not ask for these only, but also for those who will believe in me through their word, that they may all be one, just as you, Father, are in me, and I in you, that they also may be in us, so that the world may believe that you have sent me. The glory that you have given me I have given to them, that they may be one even as we are one, I in them and you in me, that they may become perfectly one, so that the world may know that you sent me and loved them even as you loved me. Father, I desire that they also, whom you have given me, may be with me where I am, to see my glory that you have given me because you loved me before the foundation of the world. O righteous Father, even though the world does not know you, I know you, and these know that you have sent me. I made known to them your name, and I will continue to make it known, that the love with which you have loved me may be in them, and I in them.

With the expectation that we have made ourselves ready, next we need to consider how we can be effective workers of the harvest.

CHAPTER TWELVE

Become Workers of the Harvest Revival

To think of the upcoming great harvest of souls is exhilarating for those of us who have an idea what to expect. Revival as discussed in Chapter One is a time when God intervenes in the lives of humankind and orchestrates a course correction. Clearly, as we considered in Part One of this book, the Church needs a course correction.

Discerning the Times

The days in which we live are a time of preparation for the harvest. Dr. James W. Goll, founder of God Encounters Ministries, and respected prophetic teacher and author, wrote about this in an article titled "Eight Proclamations for 5780 [2020] and Beyond," provided in part here:

> 1. It is a time of fresh restoration of righteousness.
> Righteousness is both a gift and an outworking in our lifestyle and character. This movement will be based in part out of Psalm 24:3–4, "Who may ascend to the hill of the Lord? . . . He who has clean

hands and a pure heart . . ." It will be a time when "the Spirit comes with conviction."

2. It is a time of divine interruptions. God is going to interrupt our schedules, our meetings and our appointments with His presence. The Holy Spirit is going to interrupt our good, program-based agenda's with interruptions of His divine presence. Watch out, here comes God as the Divine Interrupter and Divine Intruder!

3. It is a time when divine order will be established. Out of a season where there is the open conflict of thrones resulting in chaos and confusion, the Enemy will overplay his hand. God will use this backdrop to have the final word. This has ramifications on many fronts, from family to government.

4. It is a time of sacred assemblies and consecration. Out of need, there will be a movement of unity where there will be city-wide, state, provincial and national gatherings to seek the face of the Lord. There will be more public rallies of repentance and prayer, combined with the call to "GO therefore," over the next three years and beyond than in any previous time in Church history.

5. It is a time of cleansing from old disappointments. We cannot carry this baggage into the new era. Therefore, the Holy Spirit is initiating a movement of cleansing from old disappointments so we can come into the new with a fresh slate and without remorse, guilt and shame so we can be the "Hope Ambassadors" He intends us to be.

6. It is a time when the thief and the robber are exposed and caught. I have been given dreams where a security breach has occurred and is being exposed. Two dark demonic entities then

came and appeared before me and their names were "thief and robber." These enemies will be exposed and captured.

Then the voice of the Lord came to me saying, "It is time for My revolutionary midnight riders to appear on the scene. They will shine the light in darkness and expose the deeds of darkness."

7. It is a time when there is revelatory teaching on power and authority. As part of our equipment needed for the new era, the Holy Spirit will be teaching us the difference between power and authority and the necessity for both. The theme of the Authority of the Believer in Christ Jesus will be revisited.

8. It is a time for the beginning of the great harvest. This new era in Christendom is the beginning of the Great Harvest. Please note: I did not say the Final Harvest. But we are crossing the threshold into the Greatest Harvest we have ever known. It is time for the "Greatest Show on Earth" of signs and wonders and open displays of God's lavish love.

3 Necessary Requirements

Let me close by giving you three simple requirements that are necessary to walk in this new era and to see these proclamations fulfilled.

1. Greater focus

2. Greater flexibility

3. Greater wholeness

I trust this exhortation has stirred you to greater faith, hope and love. We see in part and know in part. This is a portion of what I see, hear and know for the new Hebrew year of 5780 and beyond![1]

Backdrop of Prior Contemporary Revivals

Tony Cauchi hosts a fascinating website that he describes as: "Home to the largest collection of digitized Revival and Pentecostal texts on the World Wide Web!" The site boasts a library of masses of revival books and Pentecostal material, including histories, biographies, and other resources to inspire, educate, and motivate us to seek God for a mighty end-time Christian revival. You can learn about the five worldwide awakenings spanning the years 1730s through 1960s and 70s.

The 20th century awakening was an era of Pentecostal and evangelical revivals that brought restoration and zeal to the Christian faith and ushered in many new converts to the Kingdom of God. There were four significant Pentecostal revival waves during this time.

The first was the Azusa Street Revival in Los Angeles that began April 1906. The second wave is known as the "Healing Revival" which occurred in the late 40s and 50s in America, which renewed hope of national revival all over the world. The third wave has been referred to as the "Latter Rain Revival" said to have originated in February 1948. The fourth wave is known as the "Charismatic Renewal Movement" which began in April 1960.[2]

It is deeply enriching to learn about these powerful waves of outpouring by the Holy Spirit. I encourage you to visit the revival library to learn more.

Characteristics of True Revival

What are the signs or evidences of revival? According to Dr. Paul Chappell, senior pastor of the Lancaster Baptist Church, and president of West Coast Baptist College, there are six characteristics of revival we should expect. In an article he wrote:

In less than one year's time, the Welsh Revival of 1904–1905 saw 100,000 people saved. This great moving of God's Spirit came through the preaching of a twenty-six-year-old preacher named Evan Roberts, who had prayed for revival for eleven years. So many were converted and evidenced truly-changed lives in such a short time span that the nation of Wales even became known for a time as "The Land of Revival."

In 1932, revival came to North China through the prayers of a single woman missionary, Marie Monsen. It is reported that as God's Word freely spread, more people were saved (one missionary estimated 3,000 in his town) in that year in North China than in any previous year.

In 1936, revival broke out on the campus of Wheaton College in Illinois. Faculty and students confessed sins of pride, criticism, and cheating, and made things right with one another. Meals slipped by unnoticed as God's reviving work continued in hearts. Gospel-preaching missions work around the world was the result.

But today is not 1904, 1932, 1936, or any other date of yesteryear's revivals. This is 2018, and I long for the reviving work of God among His people once again.

I know of no greater need for our nation, our church, or my own life than revival. Indeed, I know of no greater need for God's work anywhere in the world than revival.

As Leonard Ravenhill said, however, "As long as we are content to live without revival, we will."

We can go on day after day, year after year, stating our desire for revival but being content to live without it. Or we can ask God for a holy discontent for anything less than His reviving work in our hearts and through our lives.[3]

175

I pray in all earnestness for a holy discontent for anything less that God's intervention in our hearts to take place in a glorious revival in our day. The Bible speaks a lot about the great end-time harvest of souls, and many, myself included, believe it is poised to start very soon.

What can we expect to experience? Let us consider in an overview the points Chappell makes with his clever acrostic R-E-V-I-V-E:

1. Repentance: Revival is the result of a humble heart—a truly broken heart before God over sin. This is when we call the self-life, self-focus, and ongoing pride in our heart what it is—sin. And sin always separates us from God.

2. Exalt Christ: A revived heart has an overwhelming desire to exalt Jesus more than anything else—even more than the idol of self. A revived heart sees Christ high and lifted up. When Revival comes the only topic will be Jesus.

3. Value Christ: What we seek first, reveal what we value most. Our priorities are evident in the way we live in our daily lives. When we value Christ we will not only seek Him first, but we will make His passion and mission ours. We will be busy about Kingdom business which is to reach the lost for Christ.

4. Intercede: Revivals are always preceded by intercessory prayer. Not only what we pray for, but the frequency and quality of our prayer time also reveal our priorities. The person who seeks to dialogue with God through prayer as opposed to praying as a monologue obligation, will be the one whose prayers are manifest.

5. Volunteer: Revival always results in a voluntary spirit of service for Christ. When we experience the outpouring of the Holy Spirit in Revival, we are completely thrust into truth and conviction about ourselves. We are caused to realize our self-seeking ways and in proper understanding of all Jesus

did for us, motivated by love, our only plausible response to serve Him, by serving others.

6. Evangelize: True Revival always results in lost people coming to Christ because Revival gives a renewed emphasis on the spread of God's Word and revived hearts are enlarged towards Christ and His mission. When Revival comes ministry flows from our hearts and hands. We not only love the gospel, but with believing, sincerely hearts we share it. And when that sharing is accompanied by the power of the Holy Spirit, souls will be saved in number.[4]

Responding to the Holy Spirit

Based on the historical stories of others who experienced a special outpouring of the Holy Spirit, we learn many who are in attendance at a church meeting, in the open, in a tent, or in a building, may experience the restoring touch of God. In response many physically fall under the experience, which is known as being "slain in the Spirit." Others may experience being undone by the Holy Spirit, but will not give into Him by outward expression and hold the emotions and response quietly. Others become wildly excited and run, jump, or dance for joy, accompanied by shouting.

I am rather conservative in my personal expressions. When I have been supernaturally touched by God I respond reservedly. However, the more I grow in the Lord, the more experience with Him I desire. I have seen my responses progress as a result. The first time I had a supernatural touch from God caused me to greatly weep. Another time while I was standing the unexpected touch of the Holy Spirit came upon me and I felt elated and physically felt effervescent. I felt bubbly, tingly, and energized in a most unique manner. Another time while standing and receiving prayer, I felt "dreamy" and had I not resisted the experience, I believe I would have been slain in the Spirit. Instead I carefully walked back to my seat as I was rather wobbly, and leaned back and enjoyed the touch of God as long as I could.

Others explain their experience in testimonies published on "Christians Discuss: What Does the Holy Spirit Feel Like?"

> Generally speaking, when the Spirit speaks, people recognize the message as coming from God. So the first thing I'd say is the Holy Spirit feels like truth.
>
> The Spirit is described in various parts of Scripture as fire, power, faith, peace, joy, fullness, or holiness (the seal of God's promise in and on us). All these things come from God and when the Spirit makes His presence known we usually feel at least some of these things in some way or another.
>
> In most cases in Scripture the arrival of the Spirit is followed immediately by someone speaking God's word or prophesying. The Spirit of God brings God's word, and when the Spirit inspires, it feels impossible to keep quiet about the Word.
>
> The Spirit is, truly and literally, God within us. Sometimes a person can sense the presence of a Being far greater than can be imagined; I'm sure when the Spirit touches us, He holds back a great deal otherwise we'd be completely overwhelmed.
>
> In conjunction with healing and other miracles, the presence of the Spirit is often described as "warmth," "a tingling sensation," "electrical" or "breathtaking."

Readers commenting on this blog posted the following:

I felt a warm tingling sensation that started in my head and moved to the rest of my body—similar to the sensation of taking a relaxing hot shower. This was accompanied by so many tears of joy that I had to stop singing but continued to mouth the words out of love for God. This was the first time I had ever experienced joy to the point of weeping, so it all seemed very strange. Looking around I could see others were experiencing the same tears of joy.

There is no better mental or physical experience than that of the Holy Spirit. The enormous peace and joy that engulfs your mind and body is something that's unexplainable; it has to be experienced by the believer.[5]

As that last testimony stated, experiencing the Holy Spirit is a personal, intimate, connection with God that cannot be adequately explained and needs to be experienced.

A word of caution here, in the New Testament Jesus rebuked people for seeking signs and wonders, calling them a wicked and perverse generation (Matt. 16:4). *Seeking* signs and wonders instead of God is displeasing to God—we need to seek Him. Should He supernaturally touch us, it will be to confirm Himself, and potentially be in response to prayer, as in miraculous healing. We should be seeking Jesus, asking for revival because of the condition of the Church, not for the sake of experiencing the Holy Spirit.

Another word of caution, when you see someone else experiencing the touch of the Holy Spirit and you have not, do not allow the Enemy of God to whisper in your ear that you are not worthy, or you are disqualified, or any other lie. Remember the Enemy is the Father of Lies—he cannot speak anything but lies. Instead, praise the Lord for displaying His goodness for all to see and be encouraged by. Trust the Lord to do for you what is perfectly in your best interest at the proper time.

Responding to Non-believers

When revival breaks out, there will be no denying it. The unique ways the Lord may choose to reveal Himself are as creative as He is. When revival breaks out with the Holy Spirit showing up, word will travel like wildfire. People will come from far away places to witness the revival. Believers and non-believers alike will be drawn to participate. However, as discussed in Chapter Three, the unchurched who have had serious reservations about the Church will be torn. On one hand they cannot deny their deep-seated adverse opinion of the Church, on the other hand revival seems to be demonstration of the authentic, which is what the unchurched crave.

The unchurched need to be invited. Recall in Chapter Three we learned people are very receptive to coming to church if invited. However, with all the negative notions about the Christian faith and the Church, what constitutes an acceptable invitation? Let us consider what Thom S. Rainer, LifeWay president, offered in his article, "Just Ask."

> Let's suppose, instead of 82 percent [of the unchurched being likely to attend church if asked by a friend, co-worker, neighbor or family member invited them] only half of the unchurched in America would come to church if invited. That means, out of the 135 million unchurched persons, almost 68 million would be willing to come to church. Can you imagine how many people would be reached for Christ if that happened?
>
> We who are leaders in the church must challenge our church members. When was the last time they invited an unchurched

person to church? When was the last time they offered to meet someone and show him or her around the church? The answers they give could make the difference in the eternal destiny of a person. Perhaps it is time we sounded the clarion call to invite people church. It may be that simple, and it may be that profound.

What constitutes an [acceptable] invitation? For many of the unchurched, it was a simple invitation to come to one's church. For others, it was an invitation that included an offer to meet someone at church to show them around or walk them into the building. In either case, the process was pretty basic. If we invite them, they will come.[6]

I think we need to consider the skeptical culture and how we have become suspect of potential ulterior motives. Learning from the changes in marketing tactics, relationship is key. With an established relationship, suspicion is put to rest. This should cause us to consider who in our lives do we have relationship with, whom we can invite to church? What friend, co-worker, neighbor, or family member and we ask to join us at church? Thinking about this now may generate some uneasy feelings about potentially causing offense. But I guarantee you when revival breaks out, people will readily accept invitations to see the result of the Holy Spirit coming to church.

Another consideration is the fact that people who are skeptical of the Christian faith are often attracted to the Christian community before they are attracted to the Christian message. Introducing people to the relational aspect of the Christian life in the local church community, is generally well received. Fellowship, or belonging, is something we all crave. According to an article published by *The Exchange*:

In our world people are more connected than any previous generation, yet lonelier than ever before. Social media may allow us to keep up with other people, but invitations to join communities or relational circles are the only way for people to truly connect with others.

We cannot mistake information for intimacy. We cannot mistake communication for community. Virtual relationships are not complete. To put it another way, fellowship is not truly experienced apart from actual relationships in physical time and space.

Unfortunately, Western culture is inherently individualistic. We honor the person who goes their own way and values self-reliance. This pattern has resulted in an individualistic spirituality that has fragmented the church and erected barriers for people connecting in churches.

Far too often, individualism not only becomes the silent killer of community within the body of Christ, but also the hindrance to seeing growth in our churches. Fellowship Begins with an Invitation

This begs the question: how can people be added to the local church (which involves conversation and covenant) unless they experience fellowship and community with that church? And how can they experience fellowship and community in a local church unless someone invites them? If many of our un-churched friends are ready for an invitation to church, what are we waiting on? Imagine what might happen if you sparked a movement in your church.

In his book *Evangelism in the Early Church*, historian Michael Green argued that evangelism was the prerogative and duty of every church member. Green argues that "Christianity was supremely a lay movement, spread by informal missionaries … the spontaneous outreach of the total Christian community gave immense impetus to the movement from the very outset."

In our (and similar) cultural contexts, that spontaneous outreach often involves engaging people in community, leading to gospel engagement.

The experience of true gospel community, true fellowship, is a powerful thing. Remember, simply introducing people into the relational network of a local church community can be an important aspect of their journey to the faith.[7]

Return to Our First Love

Generally speaking, the American church functions like a live theater event. The church leadership has a program for the church service which starts with worship music, followed by an inspiriting message, the offering is passed, then everyone is dismissed. People arrive, take their seats, observe the production, then leave.

There are many reasons people choose to attend church, and being part of a community is one reason. However, ask people if another reason they have for attending church is to encounter the living God, and some are unlikely to agree. They may look forward to the worship music, or the message, or simply being with other believers, but a vital encounter with God in the Sunday service is rare, if ever, in some churches. In the same way Jesus did not do miracles in His own home town because of the amount of unbelief, the Holy Spirit is not interested in showing up where He is not welcomed.

We must be revived. We must have help returning to our first love and experiencing Him for all He is worth. We have been so long without properly considering our first love that we have fallen into complacency. We need help, and this is why we must intercede and pray, asking God to revive and restore us to our first love. Intercession always precedes revival.

Be Workers of the Harvest

We know Jesus told us the harvest is plentiful and the workers are few so pray for workers of the harvest (Matt. 9:37–38 and Luke 10:2). Most people read this verse and are willing to pray for the workers of the harvest. Many people incorrectly think the workers of the harvest are the church leaders. But by reading Luke in context we see in the very next verse Jesus told His disciples to go and do the work He instructed. The next verse in the Matthew reference is Matthew 10:1 where Jesus summoned His disciples and gave them authority to do the work He did. Clearly, as Jesus' disciples, we are each one to be workers of the harvest.

Because we do not know when anyone's life may come to an end, we should view every day as urgent, and seek to partner with God to bring those who belong to Him into His family. It was well over 2,000 years ago when Jesus declared the harvest is plentiful, or ripe. Today is the day we are to be prepared as workers of the harvest. When the time is right, according to God's plan, we shall see the great end-time harvest the Bible teaches. As I mentioned earlier, revival is both a judgment and a blessing. When the Holy Spirit shows up in a major outpouring, it is God's grace allowing us to make up for lost time in the harvest we should have been involved with all along.

May what you have learned from this book engage you to relate deeper with God through faith in Christ, and demonstrate your faith through your active obedience, by the power of the Holy Spirit. Then you will be among those who in the end of your earthly life will hear, "Well done, good and faithful servant. You have been faithful over a little; I will set you over much. Enter into the joy of your Master."

APPENDIX

YOU ARE WHO GOD SAYS YOU ARE
RECEIVE IT. BELIEVE IT. DEMONSTRATE IT.

1. You are complete in Christ who is the head of all principality and power (Col. 2:10).
2. You have been crucified with Christ (Gal. 2:20).
3. You are dead to sin (Rom. 6:2).
4. You have been made alive with Christ (Eph. 2:5).
5. You are free from the law of sin and death (Rom. 8:2).
6. You are born of God, and the evil one does not touch you (1 John 5:18).
7. You are holy and without blame before Him in love (Eph. 1:4; 1 Peter 1:16).
8. You have been given the peace of God that passes all understanding (Phil. 4:7).
9. You have the greater One living in you; and greater is He who is in you than he who is in the world (1 John 4:4).
10. You have received the gift of righteousness and reign in life by Jesus Christ (Rom. 5:17).
11. You have received the spirit of wisdom and revelation in the knowledge of Jesus (Eph. 1:17–18).
12. You can do all things through Christ Jesus who strengthens you (Phil. 4:13).
13. You show forth the praises of God who has called you out of darkness into His marvelous light (1 Peter 2:9).
14. You are God's child, born again of the incorruptible seed of the Word of God (1 Peter 1:23; John 1:12).
15. You are God's masterpiece, created in Christ Jesus unto good works (Eph. 2:10).
16. You are a new creature in Christ (2 Cor. 5:17).
17. You are alive to God (Rom. 6:11).
18. You are an heir of God and a joint-heir with Christ (Rom. 8:17).
19. You are more than a conqueror through Him who loves you (Rom. 8:37).
20. You have been brought near to God by the blood of Christ (Eph. 2:13).
21. You are beloved of God (1 John 4:10).
22. You are loved by the Father the same way Jesus is loved by the Father (John 17:23).
23. You have been redeemed from the curse of the Law (Gal. 3:13).

24. You have been justified from all things (Acts 13:39).
25. You are now God's offspring (1 John 3:2).
26. You are the salt of the earth (Matthew 5:13).
27. You have been reconciled to God (2 Cor. 5:18).
28. You have been accepted by God in the beloved Son (Eph. 1:6).
29. You are kept by the power of God (1 Cor. 1:8).
30. You are free in Christ (John 8:36; Gal. 5:1).
31. You are in Christ's hands from which no one can pluck you out (John 10:28).
32. You are in the Father's hands from which no one can pluck you out (John 10:29).
33. You are an overcomer by the blood of the Lamb and the word of your testimony (Rev. 12:11).
34. You are a partaker of His divine nature (2 Peter 1:3-4).
35. You are part of a chosen generation, a royal priesthood, a holy nation, a purchased people (1 Peter 2:9).
36. You are the righteousness of God in Christ Jesus (2 Cor. 5:21).
37. You are the temple of the Holy Spirit (1 Cor. 6:19).
38. You are the light of the world (Matthew 5:14).
39. You are God's elect, full of mercy, kindness, humility, and longsuffering (Rom. 8:33; Col. 3:12).
40. You are forgiven of all sins and washed in the blood (Eph. 1:7).
41. You have been delivered from the power of darkness and translated into God's kingdom (Col. 1:13).
42. You have put off the old man and have put on the new man (Col. 3:9–10).
43. You are healed by the stripes of Jesus (1 Peter 2:24).
44. You are raised up with Christ and seated in heavenly places (Eph. 2:6; Col. 2:12).
45. You have overcome the world (1 John 5:4).
46. You are greatly loved by God (Rom. 1:7; Eph. 2:4; Col. 3:12; 1 Thess. 1:4).
47. You are strengthened with all might according to His glorious power (Col. 1:11).
48. You have not been given a spirit of fear, but of love, power, and a sound mind (2 Tim. 1:7).
49. You have Christ living inside of you (Gal. 2:20).
50. You are a holy one (Col. 1:2).
51. You are one spirit with the Lord (1 Cor. 6:17).
52. You are holy, unreproveable, and blameless in His sight (Col. 1:22).
53. You are a member of Christ's holy body (1 Cor. 12:27).
54. You have been given all things that pertain to life and godliness (1 Peter 1:3).

55. You are light in the Lord (Eph. 5:8).

56. You have been given all spiritual blessings in heavenly places in Christ (Eph. 1:3).

57. You have been chosen in Christ before the foundation of the world (Eph. 1:4).

58. You have been justified (just as if you had never sinned) (Rom. 5:1).

59. You are a branch on the true Vine (John 15:1, 5).

60. You are born of God (1 John 5:18).

61. You have direct access to the throne of grace through Jesus Christ (Heb. 4:14–16).

62. You are free from condemnation and you cannot be charged or indicted (Rom. 8:1, 32–34).

63. You have been established, anointed and sealed by God (2 Cor. 1:21–22).

64. You are hidden with Christ in God (Col. 3:1–4).

65. You are a citizen of heaven (Phil. 3:20).

66. You are at peace with God (Rom. 5:1).

67. You have everlasting life (John 5:24).

68. You are kept by God's power (1 Peter 1:5).

69. You are in Christ Jesus by God's act (1 Cor. 1:30).

70. You cannot be separated from God's love in Christ (Rom. 8:35–39).

71. You are fit to partake of His inheritance (Col. 1:12; Eph. 1:14).

72. You are part of Christ's bride that He cherishes, bone of His bone and flesh of His flesh (Eph. 5:29–32).

73. You are a king and priest unto God (Rev. 1:6).

74. You have been sealed with the promised Holy Spirit until the day of redemption (Eph. 1:13; 4:30).

75. God will complete the good work that He started in you (Phil. 1:6).

76. God is for you even when others are against you (Rom. 8:31).

ENDNOTES

Chapter One

1. Tony Cauchi, "Overview of Revival," *Revival Library* (May 2006), http://www.revival-library.org/index.php/pensketches-menu/historical-revivals/general-overview-of-revivals, accessed October 2019. Used with permission.

2. "America's Changing Religious Landscape," Pew Research Center, *Religion & Public Life* (May 12, 2015), https://www.pewforum.org/2015/05/12/americas-changing-religious-landscape/, accessed October 2019.

3. "In U.S., Decline of Christianity Continues at Rapid Pace," Pew Research Center, *Religion & Public Life* (October 17, 2019), https://www.pewforum.org/2019/10/17/in-u-s-decline-of-christianity-continues-at-rapid-pace/, accessed October 2019.

4. Michael Brodeur and Banning Liebscher, *Revival Culture: Prepare for the Next Great Awakening*, (Chosen Books, 2012), 28-29. Used with permission.

5. Al Whittinghill, "Intercession Can Avert Judgment," *Herald of His Coming* (October 12, 2019) https://heraldofhiscoming.org/index.php/49-past-issues/2019/oct19/6-intercession-can-avert-judgment, accessed October 2019, originally published by Kneemail 2011, republished with permission *Herald of His Coming*, October 12, 2019). Used with permission.

6. Rich Carmichael, "Pray and Prepare for Revival!" http://www.heraldofhiscoming.com/Past%20Issues/2013/July/pray_and_prepare_for_revival.htm, accessed October 2019. Used with permission.

7. John Piper, "What is Revival and Where to We Find It?" *Ask Pastor John,* (March 10, 2017) https://www.desiringgod.org/interviews/what-is-revival-and-where-do-we-find-it, accessed October 2019, © Desiring God Foundation, desiringGod.org. Used with permission.

8. "Revival Scenes by Henry T. Blackaby," Grace Online Library, https://graceonlinelibrary.org/church-ministry/revival/revival-scenes-by-henry-t-blackaby/, accessed October 2019, © 1998 International Awakening Ministries. Used with permission.

9. Paul Chappell, "Six Characteristics of True Revival," *Christian Life* (January 11, 2018), https://paulchappell.com/2018/01/11/six-characteristics-of-true-revival/, © International Awakening Ministries, 1998, accessed October 2019. Used with permission.

10. Ellen White, *Selected Messages*, vol. 1 (Washington, DC: Review and Herald Pub. Assn., 1958), 121.

Chapter Two

1. Barna Research Group, "The State of the Church 2016" (Research Releases in Faith & Christianity (September 15, 2016), https://www.barna.com/research/state-church-2016, accessed October 2019.

2. Dan Harris and WonboWoo, "Americans Surprisingly Flexible About Religion and Faith," *ABC World News Tonight with David Muir*, December 10, 2009) https://abcnews.go.com/WN/pew-studyfinds-americans-surprisingly-flexible-faith-religion/story?id=9306080, accessed October 2019.

3. Barna Research Group, "Most American Christians Do Not Believe that Satan or the Holy Spirit Exist" (April 13, 2009), https://www.barna.com/research/most-american-christians-do-not-believe-that-satan-or-the-holy-spirit-exist, accessed October 2019.

4. Hannah Goodwyn, "Are Your Tenets of Faith Intact?" *CBN*, https://www1.cbn.com/inspirationalteaching/are-your-tenets-of-faith-intact, accessed October 2019.

5. "Reasons 18-22-Year Olds Drop Out of Church, (LifeWay Research, August 7, 2007, https://lifewayresearch.com/2007/08/07/reasons-18-to-22-year-olds-drop-out-of-church, accessed October 2019.

6. "Three Spiritual Journeys of Millennials" (Barna Research Group, June 3, 2013) https://www.barna.com/research/three-spiritual-journeys-of-millennials, accessed December 30, 2019.

7. Scott Neuman, "Millennials 'Talk to God,' but Fewer Rely on Religion, Survey Finds, NPR, *The Two Way* (April 11, 2014), https://www.npr.org/sections/thetwo-way/2014/04/11/301969264/millennials-talk-to-god-but-fewer-rely-on-religion-survey-finds, accessed October 2019.

8. Rob Hoskins, "Millennials Speak for Themselves: On Faith,"

https://robhoskins.onehope.net/millennials-speak-faith, accessed October 2019. Used with permission.

9. Ibid.

10. Benjamin Sledge, "Let's Stop Pretending Christianity is Actually Relevant, Okay?" *Heart Support* (March 22, 2017), https://blog.heartsupport.com/lets-stop-pretending-christianity-is-actually-relevant-okay-ade4c00dabcc, accessed October 2019. Used with permission.

11. Nicki Lisa Cole, Ph. D., "So What Is Culture, Exactly?" Thought Co. (August 2, 2019), https://www.thoughtco.com/culture-definition-4135409, accessed October 2019.

12. Ibid.

13. Ibid.

14. G. Shane Morris, "Biblical Illiteracy Isn't Funny, It's Scary," *Break Point*, (August 2, 2018), http://www.breakpoint.org/2018/04/27641, accessed October 2019. Used with permission.

15. Ed Stetzer, "Dumb and Dumber: How Biblical Illiteracy is Killing Our Nation," *Charisma Magazine* (2014). https://www.charismamag.com/life/culture/21076-dumb-and-dumber-how-biblical-illiteracy-is-killing-our-nation, accessed October 2019. Used with permission.

16. Penny Starr, "Education Expert: Removing Bible, Prayer from Public Schools Has Caused Decline," (CNS News, August 15, 2014) https://www.cnsnews.com/news/article/penny-starr/education-expert-removing-bible-prayer-public-schools-has-caused-decline, accessed January 2020. Used according to permission.

Chapter Three

1. Jeanne Dennis, host of *Heritage of Truth* television program, interview (October 18, 2019) of Jonathan Bock about his and co-author Phil Cooke's book, *The Way Back: How Christians Blew Our Credibility and How We Get It Back* (Worthy Books, Feb 6, 2018), https://jeannedennis.com/archives/11627, accessed October 2019. Used with permission.

2. Thom Rainer, "Just Ask" (LifeWay, April 2013), https://factsandtrends.net/2013/04/08/just-ask/, accessed October 2019.

3. Joe Carter, "Why the Decline of Protestantism May be Good News for Christians," *The Gospel Coalition*, U.S. edition (May 18, 2018), https://www.thegospelcoalition.org/article/decline-protestantism-may-good-news-christians, accessed October 2019. Used with permission.

4. Ibid.

5. Octavio Esqueda, "What Every Church Needs to Know About Generation Z," *Talbot Magazine* (November 14, 2018), https://www.biola.edu/blogs/talbot-magazine/2018/what-every-church-needs-to-know-about-generation-z, accessed October 30, 2019. Used with permission.

6. Rev. Wesley Granberg-Michaelson, "Where is Christianity Headed? The View from 2019," Religion News Service, January 10, 2019), https://religionnews.com/2019/01/10/where-is-christianity-headed-the-view-from-2019, accessed October 2019. Used with permission.

7. Outreach Media Group, "6 Common Perceptions of Christians," Church Leaders (April 19, 2011), https://churchleaders.com/outreach-missions/outreach-missions-articles/138865-i-like-jesus-not-the-church.html, accessed October 2019. Used with permission.

Chapter Four

1. Saul McLeod, *Maslow's Hierarchy of Needs, Simply Psychology* (2007, revised 2016), https://www.simplypsychology.org/maslow.html, accessed October 2019.

2. Roy F. Baumeister and Mark R. Leary, "The Need to Belong: Desire for Interpersonal Attachments as a Fundamental Human Motivation," PDF (American Psychological Association, Inc., 1995), http://persweb.wabash.edu/facstaff/hortonr/articles%20for%20class/baumeister%20and%20leary.pdf, accessed October 2019.

3. Michael Lawrence, "How 'Belonging Before Believing' Redefines the Church," *9Marks Leadership* (February 29, 2012), https://www.9marks.org/article/journalhow-belonging-believing-redefines-church, accessed October 2019. Used with permission.

4. Ibid.

5. Walt Heyer, *A Transgender's Faith*, Create Space (January 13, 2015). Used with permission.

6. Pamela Christian, *Faith to Live By,* programs 9 and 10, http://hsbn.tv/broadcaster.html?b=A0217E, accessed October 2019.

Chapter Five

1.Carey Nieuwhof, "Some thoughts Why Megachurch Pastors Keep Falling," *Carey Nieuwhof Blog,* February 2019), https://careynieuwhof.com/some-thoughts-on-why-megachurch-pastors-keep-falling, accessed October 2019. Used with permission.

2. Billy Graham's Modesto Manifesto, https://billygrahamlibrary.org/on-this-date-the-modesto-manifesto, accessed October 2019.

3. Jeremy E. Uecker, "Religious and Spiritual Responses to 9/11: Evidence from the Add Health Study" (PMC, June 20, 2011), *Sociological Spectrum: the Official Journal of the Mid-South Sociological Association*, 28(5), 477–509. Soi:10.1080/02732170802206047, https://www.ncbi.nlm.nih.gov/pmc/articles/PMC3118577, accessed October 2019. Used with permission.

4. Benjamin Sledge, "Let's Stop Pretending Christianity is Actually Relevant, Okay?" *Heart Support* (March 22, 2017), https://blog.heartsupport.com/lets-stop-pretending-christianity-is-actually-relevant-okay-ade4c00dabcc, accessed October 2019. Used with permission.

5. Benjamin Sledge, "Let's Stop Pretending Christianity Is Even "Christian" Anymore," *Heart Support* (October 8, 2018), https://blog.heartsupport.com/lets-stop-pretending-christianity-is-even-christian-anymore-455f8897ba74, accessed October 2019. Used with permission.

Chapter Six

1. J. Warner Wallace, "Young Christians are Leaving the Church–Here's Why," Fox News Channel (September 9, 2018), https://www.foxnews.com/opinion/young-christians-are-leaving-the-

church-heres-why, accessed October 2019. Used with permission.

2. Aaron Earls, "Most Teenagers Drop Out of Church as Young Adults" (LifeWay Research, January, 2019) , accessed January 2020.

3 Andy Stanley, "Five Reasons People Leave the Church" (Fox News, September 2018) https://www.foxnews.com/opinion/five-reasons-people-leave-the-church/, accessed January 2020. Used with permission.

4. Carey Nieuwhof, "A Different Take on Reaching Millennials," *Carey Nieuwhof Blog* (June 2016), https://careynieuwhof.com/different-take-reaching-millennials, accessed October 30, 2019. Used with permission.

5. Carey Nieuwhof, "5 Surprising Characteristics of Churches that are Actually Reaching the Next Generation," *Carey Nieuwhof Blog* (April 2016), https://careynieuwhof.com/5-surprising-characteristics-of-churches-that-are-actually-reaching-the-next-generation. Used with permission.

6. Octavio Esqueda, "What Every Church Needs to Know About Generation Z," *Talbot Magazine* (November 14, 2018), https://www.biola.edu/blogs/talbot-magazine/2018/what-every-church-needs-to-know-about-generation-z, accessed October 30, 2019. Used with permission.

Chapter Seven

1. J. Warner Wallace, "The Rich, Historic Roll Call of Great Christian Thinkers and Scientists," *Cold-Case Christianity* (March 2, 2018), https://coldcasechristianity.com/writings/the-rich-historic-roll-call-of-great-christian-thinkers-and-scientists, accessed October 2019. Used with permission.

2. J. Warner Wallace, "Young Christians are Leaving the Church—Here's Why," Fox News Channel (September 9, 2019), https://www.foxnews.com/opinion/young-christians-are-leaving-the-church-heres-why, accessed October 2019. Used with permission.

3. Lana Vawser, "A Wave of Travail is About to Crash Into the Church to Prepare the Way for the Fear of the Lord!, *7 Mountain Underground* (September 18, 2019), https://7mu.com/blog/a-wave-of-travail-is-about-to-crash-into-the-church-to-prepare-the-way-for-the-fear-of-the-lord, accessed October 24, 2019.

4. Jeanne Dennis, *Heritage of Truth* television program, interview (October

18, 2019) of Jonathan Bock about his and co-author Phil Cooke's book, *The Way Back: How Christians Blew Our Credibility and How We Get It Back* (Worthy Books, Feb 6, 2018), interview at https://jeannedennis.com/archives/11627, accessed October 2019. Used with permission.

5. Ibid.

6. Andrew Whalen, "God Says: I am About to Visit the Wilderness," *The Elijah List* (10/24, 2019), https://www.elijahlist.com/words/textonly.html?ID=22726, accessed 10/24/2019. Used with permission.

Chapter Eight

1. Randy Newman, PhD, "Evangelizing in a World Drowning in Sexual Problems," *Bible Study Tools,* https://www.biblestudytools.com/blogs/randy-newman/evangelizing-in-a-world-drowning-in-sexual-problems.html, accessed October 25, 2019. Used with permission.

2. J. Mack Stiles, "Nine Marks of a Healthy Parachurch Ministry," (originally published on 9 Marks.org) https://www.9marks.org/article/journalnine-marks-healthy-parachurch-ministry, accessed October 25, 2019. Reprinted/used with permission.

Chapter Nine

1. Jack Wellman, "What Happens When the Fear of God is Missing?" *Patheos Christian Crier* (October 4, 2017), https://www.patheos.com/blogs/christiancrier/2017/10/04/10310, accessed October 26, 2019. Used with permission.

2. Bert Farias, "The Absence of the Fear of the Lord is Causing Too Many People to Drift," *The Flaming Herald* (December 12, 2017), https://theflamingherald.wordpress.com/2017/12/12/absence-of-fear-of-god-causing-many-to-drift, accessed October 26, 2019. Used with permission.

3. Ibid.

4. Bert Farias, "Have You Ever Heard the Cry of the Lord?" *The Flaming Herald* (December 18, 2017), https://theflamingherald.wordpress.com/2017/12, accessed October 26,

2019. Used with permission.

Chapter Ten

1. "Religion Among the Millennials, Introduction and Overview," Pew Research Center, *Religion and Public Life* (2010), https://www.pewforum.org/2010/02/17/religion-among-the-millennials, accessed October 17, 2019.

2. Barna Research Group, "Casual Christians and the Future of America," Research Releases in Culture and Media (May 25, 2009), https://www.barna.com/research/casual-christians-and-the-future-of-america, accessed October 27, 2019.

3. Ibid.

4. Ibid.

Chapter Eleven

1. Justin Holcomb, "What is Grace?" *Christianity.com* (January 23, 2013), https://www.christianity.com/theology/what-is-grace.html, accessed October 29, 2013. Used with permission.

2. Mary Fairchild. "Why Is Obedience to God Important?" *Learn Religions*, Jun. 25, 2019) https://www.learnreligions.com/obedience-to-god-701962, accessed October 29, 2019. Used with permission.

3. Andrew Wommack, "How to: Hear God's Voice," Andrew Wommack Ministries International, Inc., https://www.awmi.net/reading/teaching-articles/gods_voice, accessed October 29, 2019. Used with permission.

4. Ibid.

5. Ibid.

Chapter Twelve

1. Dr. James. W. Goll "8 Proclamations for 5780 & Beyond," (God Encounters Ministries, October 10, 2019), https://godencounters.com/8-proclamations-for-5780-beyond/, accessed January 3, 2020. Used with permission.

2. Tony Cauchi, "20th Century Awakenings," *The Revival Library*,

http://www.revival-library.org/index.php/catalogues-menu/20th-century, accessed October 29, 2019. Used with permission.

3. Paul Chappell, "Six Characteristics of True Revival," *Christian Life* (January 11, 2018), https://paulchappell.com/2018/01/11/six-characteristics-of-true-revival, accessed October 29, 2019. Used with permission.

4. Ibid.

5. Peg Bowman, "What Does the Holy Spirit Feel Like? (Getting Started, Exploring Faith, Ministry, and Life in General, September 13, 2009), https://getstarted.wordpress.com/2008/09/13/what-does-the-holy-spirit-feel-like, accessed January 2020. Used with permission.

6. Tom S. Rainer, "Just Ask," LifeWay Facts and Trends (April 18, 2013), https://factsandtrends.net/2013/04/08/just-ask, accessed October 29, 2019.

7. Ed Stetzer, "Strategic Evangelism: The Power of an Invitation," *Christianity Today,* The Exchange with Ed Stetzer (July 21, 2014), https://www.christianitytoday.com/edstetzer/2014/july/power-of-invitation-our-god-pursues-lost-and-so-should-we.html, accessed October 29. 2019. Used with permission.

About the Author

Pamela Christian's ministry began in the early 1990s serving as teaching/director for Community Bible Study, an independent, interdenominational, international organization. This was followed by invitations to speak across the country for various organizations, which she continues to enjoy with great enthusiasm to this day. Her initial writing work included the development of workbooks for her retreats and conferences. This soon expanded to publication in book compilations, magazines, and several e-books.

Her speaking and writing career translated perfectly into other media, including hosting talk shows on Christian radio, television, and voice-over work. August 2017 Pamela was ordained as an itinerant international minister. In 2018 she was elevated to apostle and received an honorary doctorate from the HSBN International Fellowship of Ministries in association with the Holy Spirit Broadcasting Network. She earned a certificate in apologetics from Biola University, is a board member of Advanced Writers and Speakers Association, and a member of the International Society of Women in Apologetics.

Her first passion is to help others in matters of faith. Her favorite pastimes are food, family, and friends. Weekends, when she is not speaking or writing, you will find her cooking and entertaining—expressing her second passion for food, wine, and travel.

Pam and her husband live in Orange County, CA, with their two grown children and families living nearby. To book Pam to speak, or to learn more, visit www.PamelaChristianMinistries.com.

Get the other books in the

FAITH TO LIVE BY BOOK SERIES

Examine Your Faith!
Finding Truth in a World of Lies
(Revised 2015)

Renew Your Hope!
Remedy for Personal Breakthroughs
(Revised 2015)

Revive Your Life!
Rest for Your Anxious Heart
(2017)

Prepare for the Harvest!
Confidence in God's End-Time Promises
(2018)

To be sure you do not miss the release of all Pam's books, events, and more, sign up for her bi-monthly newsletter.

www.pamelachristianministries.com
Pamela Christian Ministries
18032 Lemon Dr. #C206, Yorba Linda, CA 92886
info@pamelachristianministries.com

OTHER TITLES BY PAMELA CHRISTIAN:

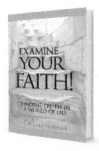

Well-meaning people want to believe all roads lead to the same God and heaven. But wanting something to be true is far different from truth lining up with reality.

- What is truth?
- Is it relative or absolute?
- Is it personal or universal?
- What are the differences among the various religious faiths? Can they be blended?

This book will help you possess a confident faith that will sustain you in any life adversity.

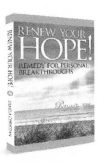

This book provides the answers that can change your life, your circumstances, and your future.

- Learn the fullness of what Christ offers you.
- Uncover the deceptions that have prevented you from moving ahead.
- Discover Christ's authority and power that God wants you to operate in.
- Take hold of the abundant, victorious life Christ died to provide you.

You can have confident hope. You can have personal breakthroughs. Why wait a moment longer when this book places the answers in your hands?

The world is in chaos, causing people to ask:

- Is mankind the supreme authority over world events?
- Does God exist, and if so what is His character, will, and intentions for the world?
- Where can I find peace and rest for my soul?
- What are my life's meaning and purpose, and how can I make a significant impact for the better in the world?

The impact you long to make *is* possible. *Revive Your Life! Rest for Your Anxious Heart,* is written so you can become all you were meant to be.

TO ORDER COPIES OF THIS OR ANY OF PAM'S BOOKS:

If you liked this book of Pam's, you will like others to keep or to give as gifts. Order at the website www.pamelachristianminstries.com, or use this form to order by mail.

Name:_____
First and Last

Shipping
Address:_____
Street and Suite/Apartment number if applicable

_____
City, State and Zip

Phone
Number:_____
Area code and number

Email
Address:_____

Please be sure to provide a phone or email address in case we have any question about the proper fulfillment of your order.

TITLE	RETAIL	QUANTITY	TOTAL
Examine Your Faith! Finding Truth in a World of Lies	$16.99	_____	_____
Renew Your Hope! Remedies for Personal Breakthroughs	$16.99	_____	_____
Revive Your Life! Rest for Your Anxious Heart	$16.99	_____	_____
Prepare for the Harvest! Confidence in God's End-Time Promises	$16.99	_____	_____

TOTAL: $_____

California residents add 8% tax $_____

Add $3.00 postage for each book* $_____

GRAND TOTAL: $_____

Shipping limited to the United States

Please send this form with your check or money order payable to:
Pamela Christian Ministries
18032 Lemon Drive #C206
Yorba Linda, CA 92886